Cradling the Chrysalis:
Teaching/Learning Psychotherapy

Cradling the Chrysalis: Teaching/Learning Psychotherapy

Mary MacCallum Sullivan and
Harriett Goldenberg

continuum
LONDON • NEW YORK

Continuum

The Tower Building
11 York Road
London SE1 7NX

15 East 26th Street
New York
NY 10010

www.continuumbooks.com

First published 2003

British Library Cataloguing-in-Publication Data
A catalogue record for this book is available from the British Library.

ISBN 0–8264–5574–3 (hardback)
ISBN 0–8264–5538–7 (paperback)

Typeset by Fakenham Photosetting Limited Fakenham Norfolk NR21 8NN
Printed and bound by MPG Books Ltd, Bodmin, Cornwall

Contents

Acknowledgements   vii

Introduction   1
1 Threads of Meaning   14
2 Teaching/Learning   44
3 'Being-Together'   65
4 The Frame for Teaching/Learning   85
5 The Substance of Teaching/Learning   111
6 An Ethical Endeavour   144
7 After Theory   165
Postscript   181

Bibliography   183
Index   191

We dedicate this book to Edith Diva Dorothy; the late Patricia Theresa Gay-French; Denis, Rohan and Emma

Acknowledgements

Together we thank Robin Baird-Smith for the opportunity of the book, and Geraldine Creaven, who deserves a medal and has our heartfelt thanks for turning hours of garbled conversation into intelligible dialogue, as does Elizabeth Stuart, who undertook additional transcription.

I would like to acknowledge and offer thanks to: David Pilgrim who taught me the power and wisdom of self-discipline, and what it means to trust in the capacity of the learner; to Leon Kleimberg who facilitated so much personal learning and from whom I imbibed so much of the craft; to Ernesto Spinelli for a great deal, in this instance, for your long-standing interest and active support; to clients and students – you bring me so much profound learning and constantly reinvigorate my enthusiasm for and belief in the process; to colleagues whose teaching is such a learning for me, and to friends who have remained tolerant and patient throughout the project.

To John, for your unfailing belief in the collaboration and in me, for your enormous generosity of spirit throughout. Your patience, tolerance and active support have been sustaining; for withstanding your first taste of an 'author' in the household – thank you, my love.

To Mary, thank you for conceiving of the idea and anticipating that we would be the right pair for the undertaking. Thank you for four years of 'oh-so-stimulating' conversation, for your skill, your energy; for your unceasing devotion to our work. Our collaboration will remain with me as an instance of true meeting.

Harriett

I would like to acknowledge those who taught me so much: David Livingston Smith, who has made significant connections between communicative psychotherapy and other disciplines, including evolutionary and cognitive psychologists, and with the work of modern philosophers of science; Carol Holmes, who showed how a communicative psychoanalytic approach can encompass the fundamental concerns that are addressed within an existential philosophical framework. I thank all my colleagues at the School of Psychotherapy and Counselling – Ernesto Spinelli, John Waller, Ian Jones-Healey, Teresa Norman, Geraldine Creaven, Adrienne Baker, Simon du Plock, Nicola Diamond, Mike Harding, Brett Kahr, Maria Luca, Lucia Moja-Strasser, Rosalind Pearmain, Freddie Strasser – who gave, and continue to give me their trust and the opportunity for unparalleled learning. From my colleagues on the Intensive Foundation course, Harriett, Carole Grace, Yiannis Arzoumanides, and on the original Foundation course, Linda Cundy; I have gained enormously in my understanding and respect for their diverse approaches and the quality of their contributions, and for the amazing experience that I have had of working with them as a team. I also acknowledge the immense learning from all clients and students, past and present, who have given me so much more than I can ever repay – they know who they are!

To Harriett I owe grateful thanks for the wonderful collaboration, for her forbearance, for her inspiration, and for the many times when she picked me up and carried me over the many

Acknowledgements

obstacles encountered. Theo deserves a mention, too, for putting up with many (for him) tedious sessions when his needs were set aside while we talked and talked (and talked)!

Mary

Introduction

Collaboration

This book is being written at a time when we're told we're at 'war with terror'; when the backdrop to our everyday existence is a heightened degree of anxiety, fear, and concern for the future of our world. This is a time when fundamental questions about what it is to be human and in relation come to the fore. We are at a 'significant time in history', yet perceive ourselves, as individuals, as vulnerable and powerless. Events in the world seem so far beyond our grasp and control while at the same time we feel deeply affected by the decisions and actions of others. Our personal power-base seems limited – consisting of our own immediate matrix of family, friends, colleagues, neighbours – and even then we feel restricted and impinged upon.

The authors are steeped in a philosophical tradition that suggests we are always in relation, but at the same time, being in relation is clearly our greatest human challenge – a challenge that is fundamental to the psychotherapeutic endeavour, and thus to our immediate concerns in this book. We cannot speak to the international context, yet we feel that it is permissible to say that in our work as psychotherapists we seek to address this sense of powerlessness and impotence at the 'micro' level of our interactions as individual humans with individual others.

1

Psychotherapy is a collaborative enterprise, and this book seeks to honour that approach.

Yet the fact of our collaboration seems in itself to have been of interest. We have been asked about it many times, by friends and other colleagues. There have been expressions of mild curiosity, serious interest, and bafflement. 'How will it work?'; 'How will you do it?'; 'In my experience one author must take the lead'; 'But your approaches and theoretical outlooks are so different'; and so on.

Perhaps, then, there is something of value, not simply in what we have to say (we hope!) but also in the collaborative fashion in which we say it. In therapeutic terms the distinction between 'process and content' comes to mind.

Indeed we have discovered a shared starting point for our separate journeys towards this task, of having always had the ambition and personal need to confront and engage with the world around us, the polity, the social, legal and political system. One author from a Jewish background, instilled with the ethical precept of *Tikkun Olum*, the Hebrew injunction to 'repair the world', to play one's part in the creation of 'heaven on earth'; the other in the parallel Christian understanding of 'kingdom theology', which encourages the individual to be active in the world, to bring about the 'Kingdom of God' in the here-and-now. These values remain strong in both of us, in the determination to engage ethically with the world, to attempt to use to the fullest extent our own selves while we are here; and to address our reparative endeavour to the smallest unit in society – the individual in relation.

The history of our collaboration is quite simple. We began as professional colleagues with differing levels of responsibility, developed a strong respect and liking for each other, recognized in each other an energy, passion, and devotion to our work, to students, and worked well together as part of a teaching team. In other words our relationship has from the outset been one of collaboration.

H: With that background Mary approached me with the idea of the book. Having collaborated on two shorter pieces with other authors, I was excited by the prospect of another co-operative undertaking. I find collaboration an exciting and exhilarating process. It is stimulating, motivating and awakening: the shared project – the brainstorming and debating, the shared responsibility to the project, and to each other. Collaboration, in itself, offers the opportunity for 'meeting'; is yet another milieu for grappling with the very personally demanding struggle to be in relationship – to engage with, to take the time to really hear, and to respond to each other. At times in our collaboration, Mary and I speak with a shared voice, at other times individually (bi-vocal). Martin Buber speaks of 'two beings set at a distance'; Erich Fromm warns of the human desire to 'merge'. We do not want to deny our separateness, our individual styles and distinct psychotherapeutic orientations. If anything we hope this book is a celebration of difference – a respect of 'otherness' – a weaving together of ideas and values and styles.

M: For me the process of working together, both in teaching and in the development of this book, has been a joy and a constant and necessary source of stimulation and inspiration; it feels so much more 'in the world' (and certainly more productive!) than to be wrestling only with myself. I engage with an 'other', with whom I can be in relation, and to whom therefore it becomes possible to offer my thoughts, hoping (and finding) that they will be heard and responded to in a way that I, in my turn, can hear

H and M: Psychotherapy is nothing if not 'a particular sort of conversation' – a dialogue where what develops does so from the

'between'. We therefore see a collaborative approach which eluci-
dates differences and commonalities between two different voices
as offering a more representative contribution. We consider that
what emerges is illustrative of a currently developing unanimity
about the intersubjective nature of the psychotherapeutic
process.

> In the most powerful moments of dialogue where in
> truth 'deep calls into deep', it becomes unmistakably clear
> that it is not the wand of the individual or the social, but
> of a third which draws the circle round the happening.
> On the far side of the subjective, on this side of the
> objective, on the narrow ridge where I and Thou meet,
> there is the realm of 'Between'. (Buber, cited in
> Goldenberg and Isaacson, 1996: 124)

Yet it seems inadequate to have this conversation on the page.
We are inevitably restricted, as are all authors, by the awesome
finality and simultaneous lifelessness of the written word; such
a stark contrast to the teaching/learning involved in becoming a
psychotherapist, which is a profoundly 'lived/felt' process.
Martin Buber uses the notion of 'speaking' as a metaphor for
the manner each of us has of relating, of communicating in the
broadest of senses. So this is the manner of 'speaking' afforded to
us at the moment – bear with us.

The particular sort of conversation between us is also a conversation between theoretical orientations, two professional 'labels',
two (theoretical) languages, two cultures, two mindsets. We two
are as different, and as similar, as any other two individuals who
meet and discuss a matter about and towards which they hold a
passion in common. Thus the hope and the intention of this
conversation is that something of truthfulness (*not* 'the truth')
will emerge from the exchange. There is no claim in this to

'know' the 'what' of which we speak; our claim is to have engaged with the 'how' – the process of 'teaching' and of writing – and to seek to communicate, out of that experience and out of our need to understand, our passion for the undertaking of an ethical therapeutic practice and training towards that practice.

M: I feel passionately about the purpose, nature and process of what has become a professional training in psychotherapy and counselling. Yet precisely that definition of the endeavour in which we both are engaged itself raises the fundamental question of what psychotherapy is and how it can be 'taught'. There is no one way, no 'right' way, even to define psychotherapy, never mind to teach it. Thus, to offer only a singular view in this field I would perceive as neither effective, nor particularly constructive in a necessarily ongoing debate about the nature of psychotherapy itself and, therefore, about what constitutes a 'professional' psychotherapy training.

In offering a binocular perspective it is important that we describe the instrument; as language shapes meaning, so does a 'theoretical orientation' shape ideas of training.

M: (Communicative) I think about therapy within an object- (or subject-) relational psychoanalytical framework, and conceive my therapeutic work (and, for that matter, my teaching) from within that mindset, together with the communicative approach to psychotherapy, which is predominantly a theory of practice. I was attracted to this approach because it seemed to offer a mode of 'validation/non-validation', from within the therapeutic inter-action, of my own contribution to the conversation, a possibility of a reliable and systematic monitoring of my practice. That it also imposes a near-impossible discipline of non-intervention and 'vigilant passivity' speaks more to my personal style and proclivities than it does to any proven efficacy of the approach. I am also clear that to follow such an approach in one part of my professional life requires, in the interests of balance, that I undertake other activities which allow me to 'perform' more actively. This, therefore, constitutes a health warning to the reader!

H: (Existential-phenomenological) To describe my orientation is a difficult task. Maybe that makes me truly existential! For me, existential concepts provide an adequate identification and description of how we humans are in the world, and of the ultimate issues we must all engage with; and within the bounds of my own understanding, I would call myself a phenomenologist. Acute powers of observation, the ability to notice, to comment in an open, and unguarded fashion – 'to say what you see', and to have the courage to 'make the implicit explicit'. I see these as crucial, difficult (yet enjoyable) elements of my task. The existential-phenomenological approach provides the pivotal bridge for me between ethical Judaism and the practice of psychotherapy.

Theoretical concepts from a range of orientations are highly relevant and descriptive of particular moments in the therapeutic process, while the lives and writing of people such as Victor Frankl, Martin Buber, and R. D. Laing bring strong resonance, profound challenge and inspiration to constantly be more present, less guarded, more alert, more disciplined, more imaginative, more compassionate. Ultimately, my time with clients is an ongoing attempt to 'be with', to enter into dialogue and to 'meet' the Other – an intensely personal endeavour.

How do our different psychotherapeutic orientations sit side by side? It's an interesting question, but much of the time, our ideas and our way of thinking go beyond that particular question to a central question within the psychotherapeutic world of how to view the spectrum of approaches at this stage in the profession's history.

Two women – is there something to say about that? The authors have taught together, we have things we would like to say about teaching psychotherapy. This is not a feminist treatise. But on reflection, of course, it is not that simple. We are two strong women collaborating. Inevitably our views on teaching, and our inclination to present our ideas through a collaboration, are influenced, perhaps even bounded, by our gender.

It seems we bring an innocence – perhaps a naïvety, and a comfort to this process. It may be worth considering what this collaboration is all about for us, to what extent it is a demonstration of the personal challenge each of us constantly takes on. Collaboration can, of course, be a tricky undertaking, as can any intimate relationship – including the psychotherapeutic relationship.

What does collaborating involve? To be able to communicate accurately and constructively, to share ideas, to stand one's ground on occasion without fear of being overshadowed or ridiculed, or without fear of potential conflict within the enterprise; to recognize where compromise is valuable while not compromising to the writing as a whole – even more crucially, to be able to get beyond conflict, hurt, misunderstanding, competitiveness, and all the other undermining, separating qualities we each inevitably bring to this project. As well as posing many challenges, this collaboration has provided the umbrella for a shared responsibility, and the space for a 'larger' vision. It has opened up what is inclined to be a very lonely process.

This shared venture, like any other shared undertaking or creation, has offered the potential for a deepened understanding between us. In the book we speak of teaching as modelling, that is, of seeking to embody in our actions and behaviour what we recommend as 'good practice' to trainees. Here too, in this book, we hope to demonstrate what can emerge from mutuality, exchange, dialogue and meeting while recognizing that what has emerged in this instance is only one of the possible books that might have been. Ultimately this project has been a grand adventure, as is teaching, as is each meeting in the consulting room.

The Book

Throughout this book, we are aware of the 'fractal' principle that 'everything is always in everything else': each chapter will be found to contain aspects of every other chapter, while each is organized around a particular theme.

Definitions of psychotherapy abound, and yet it remains an important question for those wanting to embark on training, and for those on the other side, hoping they can provide the necessary teaching. At the outset of the book we discuss some of the important aspects of the question 'What is psychotherapy?', including how it sits on the spectrum – 'Is it an art or a science?'. Recognizing that psychotherapy has a history of over a hundred years, we highlight some of the giants of the profession who have contributed to the authors' understandings of the potentiality of the work; building on their legacy, we hope to weave our own 'threads of meaning' into an ongoing conversation. In Chapter 3, '*Being-Together*', and Chapter 7, *After Theory*, we offer our views about what lies at the heart of the therapeutic endeavour.

Therapy and therapy training are clearly intricately intertwined. Is there any other field for which the training requires such intense personal scrutiny and heightened self-knowledge? With this thought in mind we consider the parallels and distinctions between the practice of psychotherapy and the training to become a psychotherapist.

The 'dialogic' model of the teaching/learning undertaking as expressed by Paulo Freire's (1972) model of 'liberation

8

education' is central to our thinking about the style of learning involved in the psychotherapeutic training process. This model places teacher and learner as equal partners in a complex inter-active relationship of 'teaching' and 'learning', rejecting the teacher as 'expert'. This dialogic style is particularly relevant to the field of psychotherapy, but of course speaks to teaching in general, and to the learning potential that exists in all our encounters with others. While delving into the processes involved in teaching and in learning as they sit side by side impacting on each other, we go beyond the particular situation of training to consider what it is to embody a dialogic style of engagement as a way of being.

The 'being-together' of therapist and client is at the heart of the therapeutic process, and yet remains the most difficult aspect of the work to grasp, and to speak or write about. In Chapter 3 we attempt to convey some of our understanding of what it is to 'be-together' both as therapist-with-client, and teacher-with-learner.

With reference to the work of Martin Buber and of Medard Boss, we share our thoughts about the potentiality of the 'meeting', which takes place between persons – one wholly embodied being together with another, whether in the thera-peutic setting, the teaching/learning setting, or elsewhere.

We undertake this description cognizant of the fact that we are entering alien territory for the traditional psychoanalytic reader. The notion of a 'with-world' is at the core of existential thought, while the language of psychoanalysis does not take kindly to discussion of 'being-together'. Or is that the case? We consider the current transitional period within the psychoanalytic sphere. The 'new' psychoanalytic psychotherapy is re-visioned as an intersubjective encounter, proposing that therapist and client are inter-related, interdependent, co-creating each other and the analytic experience.

Psychotherapy training does not take place in isolation from its context, whether this relates to the individual or to the social and global context within which we all live. In Chapter 4 we consider how the practice of psychotherapy sits alongside other forms of 'work' at the beginning of the 21st century. We embark upon an important, topical, if controversial discussion about the 'professionalization' of psychotherapy, and the implications of this for the training of its practitioners.

The immediate context for the learning is the individual training body. We explore the contradictions and dilemmas of the psychotherapy training institution, whose primary responsibility is to provide a 'safe-enough' environment, providing a 'cradling' that will facilitate the unfolding of trainees' reparative and learning capacities, and preparation for their eventual engagement with clients. The training organization retains ultimate responsibility for its alumni throughout their practice in the field, so that, while training may be a significant but relatively brief period in a practitioner's experience, the relationship between learner and institution is life-long.

The nature of all human organizations is that they often struggle to retain the freshness of the founding vision: 'politics' – that is, group dynamics and self-protective strategies – tend to come into play to subvert the 'primary task'. There will be dissonance between actual modes of 'being-together' and the organization's manifest stated ethos and values, and we discuss how this should be the subject of ongoing reflection. Further than that we offer the kernel of a vision of an institution operating along the dialogic principles we have outlined earlier in the book.

What are the 'essentials' of a psychotherapy training? We suggest that the psychotherapeutic mode of being includes the development of alertness to being, awareness of self and other that allows a sense of interpersonal process, the rhythm of active speech and an even more active 'passivity' of listening: to develop the courage and generosity to offer oneself and one's presence as the context in which the Other speaks, but to hold oneself still to 'allow' the discourse of the Other.

By Chapter 5 the reader will realize that we prioritize the interpersonal over the theoretical, but theory remains a central part of the learning. At times the task of the teacher is to help trainees to learn a language for thinking, to allow a choice of language, rather than necessarily impose their own. We acknowledge the therapeutic aspects of therapy training for the individual, and the usefulness of training as a contribution to a creative life.

Ethical precepts are intrinsic to any attempt at 'being-together' with an Other, irrespective of context. With reference to the practice of psychotherapy, it is incumbent upon teachers and learners to scrutinize their motivations, their capacity to 'hold' another, their ability and willingness to combat their own self-interest in order to be-for another – a very tough task. We discuss the intricate relationship of the elements of love, justice, power, and responsibility which underpin our engagement with others, be they learners, clients, our families or 'strangers'. We speak of an attempt to balance the responsibility of the therapist and the teacher to respect the freedom and autonomy of the client/learner, without limiting the possibilities of the process, with its ineffable magic and mystery which defy prediction and description. Once again we suggest that the learning is largely by demonstration. The challenge remains for teachers to attempt to embody the ethical values of which they speak.

What comes after theory? In the final chapter of the book we discuss the role of theory in the practice of psychotherapy in the 21st century, what value it offers practitioners and the ways in which one needs always to be vigilant so that theory does not come before and between the engagement with the person in the other chair. We consider the complexity of teaching/learning theory, and the relative significance of theory within the field.

Having highlighted the radical, (r)evolutionary nature of an ethical psychotherapy, and, by implication, the learning involved in becoming a psychotherapist, we go on to discuss the broader value of this learning.

Dialogue and Collaboration

M: When you and I were working together as members of a team, it seemed to work relatively effortlessly. It was delightful to be saying different things, but in the same place, sitting together, aiming for roughly the same kinds of outcome. If we can do that how can it be conceived of as such a difficult task?

H: Exactly. Then the book itself – as we figure out the order of the chapters, I consider they all want to sit side by side, not one after the other. Hopefully they can flow into each other quite nicely but in actual fact it's not about one coming first and then the other, it's actually about ...

M: ... the whole thing coming together.

H: It's an interesting little replica of the practice of therapy, and what we are teaching. When we teach 'skills', we say: 'We juggle with the differentiation between process and content, our own thoughts, reflections, associations, in parallel to the client's material, at the same time as we're listening and paying attention to body language, with an awareness of the frame hovering in the background. We say to students: "Don't worry about how confusing this may seem, because this is actually what happens all the time anyway, simultaneously, rather than one after the other; what we're doing is disentangling the strands ..."'

I guess we would want to say to the reader, 'Dip into any

chapter as you feel inclined. It will, by and large, all be there'; each chapter will be a microcosm of the whole book.

M: But we are all subject to the linearity of time. As we look at a painting, we have an experience (for some people, maybe not for all), which, to some extent, has to be transposed or translated into language; we can only utter one word after another, in certain patterns that allow our auditors to follow our thinking and discern our meaning . . .

H: And as we talk about what goes on in therapy, we would want to acknowledge that it can only be partial; we cannot adequately represent the ineffable. That's something we will have to live with, as will our readers . . .

Disclaimer

Both authors have studied, taught and worked in the School of Psychotherapy and Counselling at Regent's College. Clearly this experience held in common has been, and continues to be, influential for both of us, but we are in no way qualified to speak for the school, and the views and opinions set out in this volume are our own personal perspective and should in no way be taken to represent those of the school.

Throughout the text, the therapist/teacher is generally referred to in the female gender, while clients and learners are referred to in both genders. This usage simply reflects the experience and standpoint of the authors.

1
Threads of Meaning

> Fundamentally the art of psychotherapy is in weaving
> and gathering threads of meaning from words into
> experiencing, from experiencing into words. The threads
> have to be fine and capable of unravelling or holding
> powerful feelings. The threads have to emerge out of
> inchoate ground of repetitions, stucknesses, feelings and
> 'unthought knowns' which are glimpsed in many subtle
> ways. The threads are woven between both therapist and
> client. They spread from and to the world outside the
> room, but this is in a way less visible to view. Such
> threads form worlds of meaning. (Pearmain, 2001: 11)

It is an honour and a privilege to be a psychotherapist – as
practitioners and teachers we are 'on our honour' – to be
involved in the lives of others in an intimate and significant way.

What is Psychotherapy?

Psychotherapy seems to be useful, in a still-mysterious way, as a
means of combating the anxiety and powerlessness we feel in a
world which has lost its magic. Freud described the basis for
human health as the capacity and the opportunity 'to love and to
work'.

> Freedom, though it has brought [modern man]
> independence and rationality, has made him isolated and,
> thereby, anxious and powerless. This isolation is
> unbearable and the alternatives he is confronted with are
> either to ... unite himself with the world in the
> spontaneity of love and productive work or else to seek a
> kind of security by such ties with the world as to destroy
> his freedom and the integrity of his individual self.
> (Fromm, 1960: x, 18)

Ties of national, cultural or religious identity provide our sense of 'belonging' to a group, defining 'sameness', 'difference', 'relatedness' and 'otherness', binding us to the world in a particular pattern of affiliation. The accident of birth may determine whether or not we have the freedom to experience the spontaneity of love and productive work. Psychotherapy as a discipline makes the bold claim of addressing the challenge of changing patterns which bind us to non-reflexive, self-protective ways of relating, of facilitating the capacity to bear the anxiety aroused by the awareness of our human freedom, however masked by individual circumstances.

Psychotherapy also seeks to redress the ills that flow from our present context in 'an age of anxiety'. The threads of personal connection between people have been attenuated and diminished by the loss of certainty in 'traditional' models of identity, by the increasing permeability of geographical and ideological boundaries, and by the sheer weight of numbers of the human population. The forces of centralization and economic efficiency, married to the Cartesian dichotomies of the western 'Enlightenment' intellectual heritage, have brought about a de-personalizing of the human subject.

As our understanding of the nature of the therapeutic relationship has developed over the first century of its history, we have begun, together with the Scottish philosopher John MacMurray, to recognize, as a fundamental fact of our experience, the objectivity of person – the capacity to apprehend and enjoy an independent reality. Such a capacity involves personal communion – 'that persons exist and are real through communion' (Costelloe, in MacMurray, 1935, 1992: xi). The other person exists outside and independent of, yet in relation to, me, as another subject. It is the agenda of psychotherapy, through its focus on the distinctively personal dimension of our existence in the world, to seek to facilitate a re-connection with the possibilities of personal communion and intersubjective relating.

There are, no doubt, many definitions of psychotherapy, no single one of which will suffice. We speak of 'talking therapies', a term which is widely considered to encompass the disciplines of *counselling*, *psychotherapy*, *counselling psychology*, and *psycho-analysis*, not to mention the associated and perhaps overlapping fields of *clinical psychology* and *psychiatry*.

For simplicity's sake, we will ignore the confusion of tongues, names and meanings, and refer only to *psychotherapy*.

Asked the common question, 'Is psychotherapy an art or a science?', **H** has a very quick and simple response: 'Undoubtedly an art. What it has in common with science is an attempt at precision and rigorous attention to detail.' To the same question, **M** responds, 'It is both: "the imagination required by the therapist is nearer to that of the artist than that of the scientist; but he cannot turn his back on either of these disciplines"' (Lomas, 2001: xi).

H: It is an art insofar as it can never be formulaic: it is a moment-to-moment living co-creation of a relationship between two unique human beings. What takes place in the encounter between two people within (and outside of) the consulting room

16

shall always remain elusive and mysterious. Paul Gordon argues that the concern about being seen as scientific is in itself 'misguided':

> A further problem with psychotherapy is the desire, the drive to be 'scientific'. ... there is also a desire for a certain standing or status and that's a different matter. Nowhere is this anxiety about status more evident than in the debate about whether psychotherapy is or is not scientific ... Not being scientific does not mean that we are unscientific, but rather, that we are involved in something else altogether. Painting is not a science, writing is not a science, cooking is not a science, but it would be meaningless to describe them as 'unscientific'. They are rather endeavours *sui generis,* creative arts, crafts, which require their own discipline and operate according to their own rules and conventions ...
> (Gordon 1999: 26–8)

M: But psychotherapy must also take account of what might be described as 'the scientific attitude', in the belief that all human activity, including interaction between individuals, is, in some sense a natural activity, taking place within the natural order, and therefore subject to some common natural laws. MacMurray proposed that all human knowing is empirical (testable in action) if not empiricist (based only on the methods of physical science) (MacMurray, 1935, 1992).

In this view (represented by the 'Ionian Enchantment' of Edward Wilson) science is an attempt, 'on new and better-tested ground', to attain the same end as religion, that science is 'religion liberated and writ large', that the human spirit is as alive in the scientific endeavour to understand and 'liberate' the human mind as in the religious quest (Wilson, 1998).

What psychotherapists must not do is succumb to the disabling effects of an understanding of 'science' that looks for verification from an external 'objective' reality, since this encourages the tendency to 'seize upon one aspect of [our] patients and fail to recognize their wholeness' (Lomas, 2001: 85). For we are at a point in the history of the human sciences where hitherto seemingly incompatible disciplines are discovering surprising meeting points:

> ... there are interesting paths of convergence and
> coalescence arising from related disciplines that can
> facilitate our understanding of the subtleties of
> relationship, intersubjectivity, perception and thought.
> (Pearmain, 2001: 6)

At the beginning of the 21st century it is appropriate that we are no longer dictated to by the 17th-century pathologist's laboratory but rather welcome the re-uniting of body and mind complete in their social, cultural, and historic context. In fact, the scientific tool of dissection has led to the discovery of body memory and such like that corroborates the holistic nature of human functioning, experience, and expression. New technologies are illuminating the work of the human body, including the brain, as never before, and a new holism is emerging in the way we understand ourselves as interconnected with and inter-dependent on all aspects of the natural world.

However, at the same time, one cannot ignore the growing trend within science to offer 'cures' to the mysteries and agonies of existence through pharmaceuticals and the unpacking of the human genogram – at which point the conflict with a 'radical' psychotherapy becomes obvious.

And yet, in the field of psychotherapy resistance to empirical evidence is slowly diminishing: 'qualitative research involves doing one's utmost to map and explore the meaning of an area of human experience' (McLeod, 2001: viii). There is recognition of the holistic principle of 'consilience' (Wilson, 1998), and psychotherapy is open to the findings of other disciplines that may contribute to the field, such as evolutionary biology, psychology, neurophysiology, the new holistic discipline of psychoneuroim-munology, and systems theory. Thus the possibility exists of the potentiality, process and outcomes of this mysterious, clandestine enterprise being demonstrated from a scientific perspective.

Both of us view psychotherapy as an enterprise in which the therapist seeks to meet the Other in such a way as to open herself up to the Other's experience of being in the world, while maintaining a sense of her own separate groundedness in her own experience. She must demonstrate a willingness to embrace the unknown and unpredictable path ahead, eschewing the need to take charge, to take over the Other's process, or to seek to 'heal', or 'cure'. Psychotherapy is an undertaking which demands courage on the part of both therapist and client. Frequently it is described as an unreciprocal relationship. We refute this: our understanding is of a reciprocal, complementary relationship in which, in facilitating an opening up of the Other, we must seek to allow ourselves to be touched in unforeseen ways. Rather than diminishing the experience being described, psychotherapy must remain the 'obstinate attempt of two people to recover the wholeness of being human through the relationship between them' (Laing, 1967: 45).

In order to facilitate a shared experience in which the listening and creating of internal space to the Other, within the self, is the instrument and the journey. A radical openness and attunement to others (which nonetheless is securely grounded in a strong sense of oneself) is required.

Certainly in order to go out to the other you must have

the starting place, you must have been, you must be, with yourself. ... But by what could a man from being an individual so really become a person as by the strict and sweet experiences of dialogue which teach him the boundless contents of the boundary? (Buber, 1947, 2002: 24)

Such radical openness requires the creative capacity to contain and manage my own inevitable anxieties and confusion in order to be available to the Other.

> The truth is that while the therapeutic endeavour is portrayed as the journey of the client, that client's journey impinges on the therapist's. If I, as therapist, am truly to engage with the otherness of my client in his or her particularity, truly to attempt to allow my own understanding of existence to be challenged and scrutinised, then it is me, as much as my client, who enters into an uncertain, unsettling, at times terrifying, journey. (Goldenberg, 1997)

This book explores whether and how a process of training can prepare individuals for this paradoxical activity.

The 'psychotherapy wars' over the last hundred years and more (inter-theoretical rivalry, schism, competition and controversy) have sprung from, and feed on, a series of underlying psychical processes such as envy and inferiority on the one hand, and healthy curiosity, critical and creative impulses on the other. Some commentators have quoted the number of different theoretical approaches to psychotherapy as of the order of four hundred, many of which directly contradict the key tenets of others.

But currently heads are being figuratively knocked together by the expanding body of clinical research which shows that the key factor in efficacious psychological therapy is the quality of the relationship. It is now widely accepted that, whatever the theoretical stance, or professional 'label' of the therapist, whatever 'techniques' or approaches may be utilized, key factors in determining constructive outcomes of therapy are the personal qualities of the therapist and the qualities of the relationship facilitated. Theorists and practitioners from across a range of modalities are therefore engaged in exploration of the interpersonal and intersubjective aspects of psychotherapy as a generic discipline. We believe that at this point in the history of the profession divisive theory and ideology must be relegated in preference for a focus on the 'engagement' itself.

Standing on the Shoulders of Giants

Psychotherapy's history itself is an evolution beginning with Freud and encompassing the honest endeavours and best efforts of theorists and practitioners of many persuasions. We stand on the shoulders of the following heroes of psychotherapy:

Sigmund Freud, the genius from whose bold originality so much of our thinking stems or responds. He was courageous and obstinate in believing that he initiated a paradigm shift in the human sciences, and the greater part of his claim stands justified by history.

Sandor Ferenczi, in his insistent humanity and humility, took a controversial stand in support of the client who knows. His final 'Confusion of Tongues' paper offered 'blunt criticism of the superiority or "hypocrisy" of analysts who acted as though their patients were inferior to them' – an indirect criticism of Freud himself – and urged practitioners to listen more carefully: 'You will hear much that is instructive' (Masson, 1984: 294).

Harry Stack Sullivan, a prophetic voice in America in relation to his interpersonal perspective on human madness, drew on

Alfred Adler's work to emphasize the influence of the social environment in the development of schizophrenia. He showed a determination to put himself alongside his patients, and was a seminal influence on the work and development of the object-relations school in America.

Ronald Fairbairn, isolated in Edinburgh from the pressures of the incestuous metropolitan psychoanalytic community in London, broke with the Freudian and Kleinian view of the instincts as primary and anticipated the work of Winnicott and Bowlby. He proposed 'splitting' as a fundamental and universal adaptive strategy in the face of traumatizing experiences, and significantly revisioned the human infant as 'tragic', subject to the dis-appointments of ordinary human relational life, rather than culpable in its aggression and psychotic anxiety as in the Kleinian perspective.

Erich Fromm showed us 'that all [our] attempts for love are bound to fail, unless [we try] most actively to develop [our] total personality, so as to achieve a productive orientation; that satisfaction in individual love cannot be attained without the capacity to love one's neighbour, without true humility, courage, faith and discipline' (Fromm, 1975: Preface).

Donald Woods Winnicott saw one of the aims of psychoanalysis as 'to re-establish continuity with whatever constituted the patient's "personal beginning"' (Phillips, 1988: 22). He sought to make his work accessible, his language plain, and demonstrated a commitment to 'affinity between people' rather than to professional technique. He made us aware of the 'holding' aspects of the therapeutic, as of the parental, relationship so that it is the developmental process of the client that should determine the direction and pace of the work.

Victor Frankl met the 'unimaginable' and 'inhuman' head on, and straddling the lived/observed experience, discovered that even in such extraordinary circumstances where the objective is precisely to destroy the sense of humanness, the capacity to create meaning need not be lost.

Martin Buber presents us with a vision of the delicacy, potency and complexity of 'relation'; relation to oneself, to an Other, to nature, and ultimately to God. In writing that defies the boundaries of any one scholarly discipline, his poetic understanding of the potentialities of 'the dialogic' inspire and inform.

Ronald David Laing, for his courage and daring in transgressing the boundaries of received wisdom. He taught us that, if we find the madness in ourselves, the madness in others need not be so frightening. His outspoken passion and humanity, his willingness and ability to embrace the Other with an intriguing blend of strength and delicacy, wit and challenge, taught us that if we listen fully the mystique of the seemingly inexplicable dissolves.

Harold Searles is a luminous representative of Sullivan's heritage, in the vanguard of those who have shown how fruitful it is to be open to learning from the wisdom and insight of his schizophrenic patients.

Robert Langs, discoverer of a profound spring of human wisdom and poetry in the human mind and proponent of a systematic mode of 'validation/non-validation' of the activities undertaken by psychotherapists which may contribute to a 'science' of psychotherapy.

Ernesto Spinelli, a great story-teller, who gently but unceasingly challenges us to consider why we do what we do; to relinquish our desperate need to know in favour of an honest, if naked 'un-knowing'. His understanding of the 'co-constitutional' nature of existence brings us back from our isolation to the reality of mutuality and exchange.

The above, among others, made radical and original contributions. Derived from our learning from them, the authors share the belief in the immeasurable possibilities and richness of creativity in each of us, which is available as a resource for the work we do. We see this evidenced in our practice, as therapists and as teachers.

The corollary of the positive attitude we describe is the willingness to attempt to tolerate the worst that can be done by the Other to destroy, to struggle to maintain patience, strength and the capacity to contain toxicity, without being destroyed, and without having one's reparative capacities undermined.

A competent professional psychotherapist, then, is one who is consistently able to provide and facilitate a relationship in and through which a client may be encouraged to undertake a process of self-exploration and self-discovery. The therapist's primary aim is to achieve a 'being-with' the Other: to sustain a quality of attending to her client which will allow him to disclose himself to himself, whilst remaining herself relatively unknown. The development of such a relationship requires her to be at once professionally 'neutral' and yet to demonstrate in her behaviour a kind of 'love' for the client.

We must be bold enough to define and harness the wish that is expressed by applicants for professional training to 'help' others. Such a wish must be examined rigorously and remorselessly throughout training and throughout practice in order to reveal its self-serving elements. If, even after sustained examination, there is a remaining excitement about the particular form of meeting the Other that constitutes psychotherapy, together with a continuing willingness to attempt to be in a way that facilitates such a meeting, then we consider that the presence of a form of love is proved.

We must also be alert for the obverse of altruistic love: 'the more we strive to be professional helpers who have the best interests of our clients at heart, the more we are in danger of acting out of our power-hungry shadow' (Güggenbühl-Craig,

1971, 1999: xiii). Any form of professional involvement in the 'caring' industries is subject to the desire for power, and each and every action must be considered for its ethical implications, as must each individual's motivation for such a 'career' choice.

As an invention of the 'West', deriving from the values of the European Enlightenment,[1] psychotherapy is criticized from a non-Western perspective for its apparent privileging of individual autonomy above the well-being of the group (family or community). Concepts like duty (e.g. to parents or to family) and responsibility for others have, it is claimed, been devalued. Adherence to the primacy of individual autonomy in a notional league-table of values has been blamed for the decline and fragmentation of social structures, resulting in damage to the 'fabric of society'.

The authors are alert to this state of affairs. We are saddened by and reject such an isolationist model. Rather, we advocate an ethical psychotherapy which recognizes and respects the inevitable presence and impact of the broader social contexts – both ours and our clients – within the bounds of the therapeutic meeting.

> ... this way of being involves serious and earnest engagement with the multiple and intertwined relations between ourselves and our clients, our worlds and their worlds, both inner and outer ... (Goldenberg and Isaacson, 1996: 127)

1. **M**: We can't talk about Enlightenment values without thinking through the full implications for the Other of the stance thus taken. All too often, such speech merely betrays an underlying assumption of superiority to other value-systems. This assumption is based on the reality of the long-standing global hegemony of a Christian world-view. 'Globalization' may be seen as a reiteration of Christian missionary colonization, which resulted in the widespread experience of discrimination, oppression and persecution of non-Christians, including Jews, despite the crucial contribution of their history and religious insight to western ideas.

Therapy and Therapy Training – More Similar than Meets the Eye

> a meeting between two people involved in a relationship
> from which creative developments are expected ... [The
> task ... is to facilitate a shared experience in which] the
> listening and creating of internal space to the other,
> within the self, is the instrument and the journey.
> (Momigliano, 1992: xxii)

Teaching therapy and learning to be a therapist – the two aspects of the process which takes place in any therapy training – are clearly distinct but interdependent and intertwined, as are the processes of training and the practice of therapy itself.

When asked: 'How does it feel to be talking about the intangibles?', a student's response was: 'Very good – I don't often get the chance.' This simple exchange highlights the potential power and scope of the process of training, as well as its similarity to the potentiality of the therapeutic relationship.

Of course there are important distinctions between training and the practice of therapy. These, as well as the similarities, will be considered in detail, but the interconnection between the two cannot be overstated. Put simply, both processes afford an opportunity for a deep learning about oneself.

In fact, if one considers that a distinctive characteristic of being a therapist is that, as a practitioner, 'you are your instrument', it is vital that training facilitates the process both of thoroughly familiarizing oneself with oneself, and at the same time honing and developing one's capacities to be with another – so that the trainee becomes equal to the demands of the therapeutic task. While training involves absorbing a great deal of theoretical information, it also demands a dialogic style of engagement with the material which combines both intellectual and personal openness, a willingness to allow cherished values and beliefs to be challenged, and to engage with others, colleagues and teachers, as a way of learning to be with 'real' clients. The personal encounter with the fundamental ideas and questions which challenge the training psychotherapist closely parallels the demands which therapy itself makes of clients. Not surprisingly it is crucial, if contentious in some circles, that the trainee experience personal therapy as a part of the learning.

The encounter must be a lived experience, a risking of oneself to the possibility of a profound and lasting effect on how one is with oneself and with others, with the possibility of considerable, if often subtle, change which simply cannot be predicted or predetermined. If this risk is not faced with courage in the context of therapy training, it is unlikely to be fully engaged with in the consulting-room.

It is akin to the risk taken by prospective clients, whom we expect to expose themselves to the possibility (if not the probability) that, in opening up their inner world to our inquiring gaze and exploration, they may experience us as cruelly misunderstanding and judging them, when what they seek is to be understood, to be met.

As part of the teaching/learning, students are required to demonstrate their therapeutic capacities and skills, to both tutors and peers, in the service of learning and of the evaluation of that learning. Becoming a skilled therapist involves the 'un-learning' of many taken-for-granted assumptions about oneself. It involves voluntarily embarking on a process of 'un-knowing', of daring to unravel and examine the 'me' that I think I know. For each student

> Implicit in the remit of gaining greater self-awareness is the suggestion that to a greater or less extent, I am a stranger to myself. The process of coming to know myself better, more fully, is fraught with possibilities of feeling

estranged from myself. The familiar becomes unfamiliar and the unfamiliar becomes known. (Goldenberg, 1997: 13)

The necessary self-disclosure of one's own frailties as a human and shortcomings as a learner, a fledgling practitioner, in the context of the learning group, both peers and tutors, carries the risk of moments and situations in which trainees will feel 'shamed' and rejected through peer criticism and feedback. This painful experience can be seen as parallel to the self-disclosure required of clients in therapy. However, the development of enhanced and disciplined self-reflection and self-awareness must be evidenced for the purpose of the evaluation and assessment necessary to a professional training, the outcome of which is a 'licence' to practise psychotherapy with vulnerable individuals.

M: Particularly at the beginning – at the foundation level or even prior to that – people come for interviews saying, 'I know all of this; I'm capable of all of this; I don't need to start from the beginning.' These are attitudes and assumptions being expressed. It's our task in the first stage of training, to blow away the cobwebs that are these assumptions, to say 'open your mind'.

H: There is a very uncomfortable ongoing, even never-ending, process, common to practitioners, teachers and learners that takes place around sharing how frightening and unsettling it is to submit to the 'not-knowing' or to allow for uncertainty. It is that finely balanced combination of allowing uncertainty, while having an inquisitiveness that we are attempting to cultivate further. As teachers, part of what we should be trying to model is a certain amount of, not necessarily comfort, but preparedness, to be with that 'not knowing', and to resist the temptation to 'know'.

M: And this is also paralleled in therapy (although I would hate to generalize from this). Clients may come to therapy saying: 'I'm not really sure that I need therapy, but there is one particular area that I would like to look at …' That 'little area' can often turn into a radical re-appraisal of a life and a self.

Some learners come as experienced clients, and may be shaken to the core by the un-learning and new learning about themselves that the training represents. 'Well, I've done therapy; I've worked through these and these issues. I'm simply a little at a loss right now …' ('Been there; done that; got the T-shirt.') And yet, there's more to be done; there's often so much more, and at a much deeper level, that can be done.

As with learning, so with the teaching. In order to facilitate such a process in and for trainees – a heavy responsibility – I must myself be continuously open to learn and be changed in the process, as well as witnessing and containing whatever unfolds in my students. The same, again, can be said of therapist with client. The task is stimulating, joyful, moving and arduous.

Therapy training itself must assume and encourage a continuing process of self-exploration and developing self-awareness as the necessary foundation of the interpersonal skills and insights which underpin the therapeutic interaction. The demand made of psychotherapy trainees is such that their engagement with and experience of training must be susceptible to description as a therapeutic process, undertaken in a 'public' environment, where progress in both aspects is subject to constant evaluation.

Yet, paradoxically, training institutions are rightly steadfast in maintaining that therapy is not, and must never be allowed to be, the point of the training process, since the real 'object' of the exercise, in all its different modalities, is the well-being of the present and future client of the psychotherapy trainee.[2] While this clarity of purpose is vital, particularly in such a human endeavour, the reality appears to be that training and personal self-discovery are inextricably bound up together. One might go further, to suggest that all learning involves emotional as well as intellectual processes, and that we, as therapists and as therapy teachers, must be always and acutely cognizant of that fact.

Thus the parallels between the experience of the psychotherapy trainee and that of the psychotherapy client deserve to be more explicitly articulated, in order to focus on what aspects of and qualities in training constitute 'best practice' irrespective of theoretical orientation – in order to unpack both the learning and the teaching process. Those who participate in the training of prospective therapists must acknowledge the permeability of the boundary between the training and the 'therapeutic' function of the training process.

There are many elements to both therapy and to therapy training. It is useful to attempt to identify these and to consider the distinctions and similarities already alluded to, in some detail.

Structure

Any professional relationship, whether between two individuals or between individuals and an organization, is predicated on a 'contract' set up between the two parties.

The contract of a therapeutic relationship sets the parameters of that relationship in terms of the one individual obtaining a service from another; in the case of therapy training the

---

2. POPAN (Prevention of Professional Abuse Network) reports receiving many allegations of emotional, physical, sexual and financial abuse from clients of psychotherapists, counsellors, psychiatrists and counsellors (POPAN leaflet, 2001; Pointon, 2002).

agreement is with the training institution of which the trainer is a representative, the service being the provision of the necessary atmosphere in which to develop a professional competence on the part of the prospective psychotherapist.

Both of these 'contracts' entail a number of agreed elements.

The physical environment provided should, as far as possible within the usual resource constraints, model that provided for therapy. That is, it should contribute to an atmosphere of calm and privacy, with a degree of comfort and quiet – providing appropriately soundproofed seminar and practice rooms, with seating which facilitates periods of attentive listening.

The human environment in which training takes place should offer a similar model of respect for learners' autonomy: managers of training should strive for transparency in their dealings with students, and should demonstrate a willingness to be accountable for the standard of the service offered to those who undertake training, often at considerable personal and financial sacrifice. A willingness to listen to student feedback regarding the effectiveness of the training and the direction of its ongoing development should be an integral element in all programmes.

In contrast, transparency is not a word usually linked to the practice of psychotherapy. In fact this is an area of much contention within the psychotherapeutic world; the 'demystifying' of the therapeutic encounter (Spinelli, 1994) is seen by many as antithetical to and undermining of the potentiality of the process.

This is perhaps one of the more obvious points of distinction between being a learner/practitioner and a client. As a learner one is allowed 'behind the scenes' into the area of 'why' and 'how', while as a client one experiences the 'what' of the process.

No learning space can ever be entirely 'safe', however. An important element in any form of human development is an acceptance of the reality of human shortcomings. The inevitable failures of and disappointment in the training environment provide a significant 'reality test' which speaks to the limitations of all human interactions, and to the individual's responsibility for her own learning outcomes, which can never be overstated.

The competence, too, of the individual teacher can never be just 'assumed'. Anyone who claims to be a teacher must continuously attend to her own professional development in terms of her grasp of the ideas and concepts to be communicated and explained, and in terms of the learning environment provided. Attention must be paid to the differing needs of individual members of the training group, who will come with a diverse range of life experience, including cultural and religious background, socio-economic class, sexual orientation, and many other forms of 'difference'.

Training organizations should support high standards of teaching skills, and should be prepared to nurture and support the professional development of those employed for the purpose. We should also encourage consideration of innovation and experimentation in terms of teaching methods and technologies, and of the continuous pursuit of quality.

The duration of psychotherapy training is famously long-term, and generally part-time. The complexity of human nature means that the development of the 'honed' capacities and skills of an experienced and competent therapist will be a process of spiralling learning incorporating different stages. In therapy we acknowledge that predictability of time-frame may often be impossible; if one extrapolates from therapy to the process of therapy training, then any clear-cut time-frame to training also has to be questioned.

In this respect the two activities present an entirely different agenda. Psychotherapy itself should, arguably if perhaps rather naïvely, have no agenda other than that of 'being-with' the client. Yet publicly funded psychotherapy must find the means to sit within an 'evidence-based' context in which 'value for money' and 'efficacy' must be demonstrated, a demand which calls for criteria against which to measure efficacy and value. Psychotherapy training, similarly, must have clear objectives which relate to the explicit anticipated learning outcomes which have to be actively and continuously addressed throughout the course of training.

Akin to the mystique of the therapeutic process, to which the therapist may claim to be exclusively privy, therapy trainers run the risk of perpetuating the myth of secret knowledge of which they are the gatekeepers.

In an independent clinical context, particularly in most so-called 'non-directive' models of therapy, any evaluation and assessment of a client would be widely regarded as intrusive and non-therapeutic, while raising the question of the hierarchy of power within the relationship. Yet a form of client evaluation is considered necessary in public-sector psychotherapy, demonstrated in the 'intake' or 'assessment' interview, regular supervisory review of the work, and outcome evaluation, in the interests of clinical governance of the service and of effective management of public money. These practices resonate with the evaluation and assessment that take place in the training context.

The evaluation of learners' progress is central and unavoidable within any training activity; it highlights the locus of power in the unequal relationship between learner and teacher. The emotional impact of therapy training, like therapy itself, is impossible to prepare for, and this creates a gulf between the 'knowing' of the trainer and the unknowingness of the prospective trainee that fosters the inequality of power.

Clarity and transparency of criteria for the evaluation of the qualities, skills and attitudes demanded of a 'competent' therapist, achieved through a careful articulation and publication at the outset, go some way to redress this imbalance.

In addition, educators are increasingly aware of the need to evaluate their own performance. As within the practice of therapy, trainers must continually submit their practice to the scrutiny of both their students and their peers. If, as is discussed more fully later, the teacher is putting herself forward as a model, she must be prepared to monitor her teaching methods, her style and her 'presence'; criteria for evaluation of all these elements are therefore necessary.

The question of fee in the provision of psychotherapy is a contentious issue. In one view, unless clients pay their therapist a fee, however minimal and token this payment may be, they will not see the therapy as having value *for them*; they will not have wholly chosen to enter into the therapeutic relationship, and their decision to continue with therapy through 'difficult' times may speak more to their sense of lack of personal autonomy and despair than to confidence in the efficacy of the relationship.[3] Another view, informed by the principle of a 'health' service free to the client, underpins the provision of many psychotherapy and counselling agencies and critiques the unfairness and elitism of a fee-paying service which excludes many clients who could find therapy useful.

Psychotherapy training offers an entirely different paradigm: since it is, at the time of writing, almost always entirely self-funded, it is unlikely to be other than a freely chosen undertaking. Yet in most therapy training institutions there is a clear pathway through training to the point of professional registration, which, at the time of writing, is achieved through the institution rather than as an individual.[4] This bestows on the

3. This argument does not denigrate therapy that is free to the client; what it does mean is that the issue of client autonomy and choice must continually be addressed in every therapeutic context.
4. This applies to UKCP Registration only. Both BACP Accreditation and BPS recognition are based on an individual application process.

institution considerable power over the potential future livelihood and career prospects of the individual trainee.

Again, as with therapy itself, so with therapy training – many excellent potential applicants for training will be excluded because of lack of funding, which contributes to the charge levelled at psychotherapy of elitism or sectarianism. Many trainees make considerable financial sacrifices to manage the cost of this long and arduous academic and vocational apprenticeship. Where difficulties arise in the relationship between student and institution, the financial implications of these may engender perceptions in students of being unfairly treated and financially exploited. The student will be concerned with the principle of 'value for money', while the institution will be concerned to retain students as a source of income, with all the ethical and professional questions that this provokes.

It may be argued that this mirrors the potentiality for financial exploitation in private psychotherapy practice, in that individual clients paying a considerable fee constitute a proportionately large part of the livelihood of the private practitioner. This carries its own risk: the temptation, to even the most consciously ethical therapist, of finding oneself concerned at the prospective loss of a client in terms of the loss of a source of income.

In the practice of psychotherapy there may be a temptation to proceed on the basis of an assumption of our own 'goodness'. A radical respect for persons, as discussed in Chapter 6, implies an alertness to our tendency to use others for our own benefit, together with a willingness systematically to address this tendency in our dealings with others.

Individual autonomy has to do with the capacity of the individual for self-government, a felt sense of the freedom to will. In entering therapy, clients, of necessity perhaps, give up a degree of their personal autonomy to the therapist. It can be argued that clients are required to trust the therapist, in order for therapy to be effective, in order to develop 'a therapeutic alliance'. The same can be said of therapy training: the trainee gives up a degree of autonomy in putting herself in the hands of the trainer, or training institution, and must rely on the individual trainer or institution to fulfil that trust.[5]

Power (responsibility) and Vulnerability

What is at stake is our ability to be the person we want to be, rather than being the person others want us to be.
(Korda, 1975: 58)

Bearing in mind what has already been said, clearly the relationship between student and teacher is potentially a very powerful and influential one, akin in many ways to the possibilities to be found within the therapeutic relationship. While much has been written about 'power' within the context of therapy itself, particularly its potential and actual abuses, the dangers implicit within the teacher/learner relationship are perhaps less obvious.

But adults, who by virtue of undergoing such training, are at a time of personal transition, and are therefore particularly susceptible to what some would call the 'transferential' elements of the process. The teacher needs to be cognizant of this aspect of training – the need and inclination of learners, as well as their own predisposition or antipathy towards taking on a nurturing role. A relationship may be created which leads to professional and ethical questions similar to those that exist within the practice of psychotherapy.

---

5. Anecdotal evidence suggests that complaints, in relation to both psychotherapists and training institutions, stem from the 'disappointing' of this trust, a sense that the ceding of autonomy has been abused.

At the same time, teachers need to be aware of their own needs, i.e. for an audience, for a platform, for admiration. When a particular theoretical model has become 'your truth', it is easy to confuse it with 'the truth', but any therapy training which has become indoctrination has clearly overstepped the mark. The disciplined professional trainer offers a perspective, or a model of therapy, that is open to challenge.

One of the distinctions which many would draw between psychotherapy training and practice is the fact that training is overtly instructive in nature. We 'teach' psychotherapy – its theoretical basis and the skills involved in its practice – but we also must acknowledge that we do much more than that. With the exception of some cognitive-behavioural approaches, which openly view the therapist as a mentor and employ 'modelling' techniques, most 'non-directive' approaches attempt to disclaim this element of the relationship. Be that as it may, the mentoring element of psychotherapy training cannot be denied. Willingly or not, teachers of psychotherapy stand before their students as models. This is both a privilege and an onerous responsibility.

In concrete terms, teachers and training institutions hold the power and responsibility of evaluation and accreditation of trainees, affecting career, life chances and choices of prospective psychotherapists. It is thus incumbent on teachers and their institutions to exercise this power in a manner that reflects the values of psychotherapy itself, and that resonates with an acknowledgement of the individual rights of students, and with those of their prospective clients.

The responsibility of the teacher and the training institution is complex and multi-faceted: there is the responsibility towards each individual learner within the context of a group of students, the responsibility towards their anticipated future clients, as well as, some would posit, a wider responsibility towards others in the world of such potential clients, and even society as a whole. In other words, teaching therapy is a professional endeavour with a specific outcome – practitioners. This calls into question the function of training institutions with regard to monitoring/ regulating and re-accreditation of graduates. Clearly, a distinction is to be drawn here between the responsibility of individual teachers and that of the institution. That said, such a distinction is not easily made; in practice, the institution functions through its individual teachers.

At every stage the notion of balance is central. In all realms power and responsibility sit side by side – with power goes responsibility. Within the field of psychotherapy a recognition of the power of training institutions and individual teachers has to be juxtaposed with an acknowledgement and respect for the autonomy, potency and personal responsibility of trainees – adults who have chosen this path.

Holding the Unpredictable

Each therapeutic encounter is unique and unpredictable. The therapist works within structures which she must safeguard, thereby offering 'containment' (Bion) for whatever emerges in a particular session. Within these boundaries, the therapist must have the ability and willingness to innovate, to allow for spontaneity and to be prepared for the element of 'surprise'. It could be said that these boundaries are created precisely to allow for the uncertainty and unpredictability of what may take place within them.

There is a similarity with therapy training, in that, in order to be responsive to the needs of learners at a particular moment, the teacher must be alert to the possible need to forego any predeter-mined agenda, and to be guided by the pace and receptivity of the learners.

Given the potency of the material being considered, the therapy teacher carries responsibility in terms of 'holding' the tension – the stimulation, anxiety, confusion and discomfort. The teaching/learning situation unleashes a process of self-discovery. Unlike therapy itself, where the therapist primarily sits with the client's material, training presents a constant process of offerings, which often act as a catalyst for individual learners. A lecture on Freudian or Kleinian theory, for example, may provoke an unexpected internal, personal response to the ideas and concepts. An awareness of this potentiality leads to implicit, important ethical questions about the bounds of the teacher's task and responsibility.

As with the therapeutic relationship, the teacher offers an implicit optimism about humanity. It is incumbent on the teacher to 'trust' in the capacity and ability of students to learn, to develop, to process and internalize; to recognize what is her responsibility as teacher, i.e. 'holding the ring', 'maintaining the frame' – while at the same time allowing training to be what it is: an interactive process which may develop in unforeseen directions.

> **Rhythm**: Movement marked by the regulated succession of strong and weak elements, or of opposite or different conditions. (Shorter Oxford English Dictionary, 1973)

One thinks of rhythm in terms of music or dance. These provide useful metaphors to bear in mind: 'underlying tempo', 'crescendo', 'staccato', 'finale'; from performance: 'solo', 'duet', 'quartet', 'orchestral', 'synchronize', 'jam', 'improvization'. Going beyond music and dance, natural rhythm, subtle and influential, surrounds us: in the cycle of the year, the life cycle, our very personal daily rhythms, the rhythm of a conversation.

There is a rhythm, often ignored, to learning. The scope of the learning required of the trainee psychotherapist encompasses theory, experience, technique and self-awareness. These demand different modalities of thinking, and of personal engagement in concert. This combination can often be discomfiting and disconcerting, and can be experienced as both draining and/or energizing. There must therefore be a managed rhythm to the process of training – 'a regulated succession of strong and weak elements'.

Again there are parallels between therapy and therapy training. It is up to the teacher to anticipate and safeguard the rhythm of the learning, in taking care about calibrating rhythm, both pace and pitch, to the demands of the 'here-and-now' process.

> ... there is established a pattern of withdrawal and return which constitutes the universal and necessary pattern of personal development ... The withdrawal is for the sake of the return; and its necessity lies in this, that it differentiates the positive phase by enriching its content. Without the negative there could be no development of the positive ... (MacMurray, 1995: 91)

In practical terms, psychotherapy training consists of a combination of elements, as already stated, providing different learning triggers (i.e. intellectual, experiential) within different social groupings – one-to-one, dyad, triad, small group, large group – which provide the opportunity for different styles of engagement, with differing rhythms, ranging from the more private and intimate to the more public. Lastly there is the to- and fro- interaction between teacher and learner – the initiating, the responding, and the allowing for space in the middle. The shift from one to another can be managed so that, in experiential terms, there is a logical and seamless flow, recognizing the inevitability of a beginning, a middle, and an end.

Creating and Attending to Atmosphere

In the therapeutic endeavour, as in the teaching setting, responsibility lies with the therapist/teacher, firstly to create, and then to manage an atmosphere that is facilitative of learning and a process of self-discovery. This task includes not simply setting an atmosphere but also attending to it, in the sense of noticing, monitoring and engaging with the intersubjective elements of the encounter; being able to recognize (and then work with) whether your client/student is with you – or you with her/him. Heidegger speaks of 'leaping in' and 'leaping ahead', the former running the risk of taking over and overshadowing the client's/learner's process, while the latter safeguards the space and anticipates what may lie ahead.

In therapy the practitioner is always having to make judgements about the appropriate intervention: when to remain silent, judging the strength or vulnerability of the client, and so on; operating at what some would call an intuitive level, while others speak of being guided by the unconscious, and yet others speak of working with the intersubjective elements of the relationship.

A teacher, particularly of psychotherapy, needs to go beyond a simple focus on imparting theoretical information to judging and being attuned to whether the students have engaged, comprehended, digested; judging quantity and volume of information, pitching delivery at a level that can be received, judging pace and rhythm – essentially making the learning a safe place in which to question, to admit to not understanding, or to disagreeing, opening up areas of thought and feeling, rather than closing down the process. Therapy training, as therapy itself, is a lived process – hopefully a shared process between therapist/teacher and client/learner.

Magic and Mystery

How training is actually conveyed is often an elusive question. Therapy training, like therapy itself, has historically been cloaked in mystery. In recent years there has been an attempt to debunk and demystify therapy (Spinelli, 1994), as well as to regularize and standardize its component skills and competencies in the service of good practice. This latter process has been productive and illuminating, but has largely omitted to address, has in fact attempted to avoid or deny, the more 'intangible' aspects of the endeavour, whether in training or practice.

In a concert performance musicians are working within a given form, but each occasion is something more – unpredictable, unique to that rendition, full of the potential for surprise. At every stage of both therapy and training there is an element of improvization, of engagement with an intellectual and emotional climate that is the co-creation of teacher/therapist and learner/client together, uniquely in that particular moment.

When, for example, we speak of the 'presence' of the person of the therapist, or lecturer, we are giving a name to a quality of being, of relating, an atmosphere seemingly surrounding or generated by that individual, which is highly personal and unquantifiable, but, in itself, potentially therapeutic.

In our attempt to bring therapy more into the public domain, we have to be watchful that we do not overlook the qualities of the encounter between people, in this instance therapist and client, or teacher and learner, that remain beyond our grasp. As R. D. Laing says:

> True, in every enterprise of psychotherapy, there are regularities, even institutional structures pervading the sequence, rhythm and tempo of the therapeutic situation viewed as process, and these can and should be studied

with scientific objectivity. But the really decisive moments in psychotherapy, as every patient or therapist who has ever experienced them knows, are unpredictable, unique, unforgettable, always unrepeatable, and often indescribable. (Laing, 1967: 47)

2
Teaching/Learning

Have you ever really had a teacher? One who saw you as a raw but precious thing, a jewel that, with wisdom, could be polished to a proud shine ... (Albom, 1997: 192)

The metaphor of 'cradling' we have used in the title of the book speaks to the function of the teacher as we understand it, that sense of delicately holding, which safeguards, strives to facilitate, while endeavouring not to squeeze, cramp, rush or mould the potentiality of the learner. 'Holding' the learner includes not only the quality of a teacher's 'presence', together with the physical arrangements and the total environmental provision, but also describes a three-dimensional relationship which includes time and 'space' (room to grow). Holding seeks to make tolerable and manageable the inevitable developmental 'dis-appointments' (Fairbairn) and 'insults' (Winnicott; see Grotstein and Rinsley, 1994).

To be human means to be 'hard-wired' to learn; yet we know that curiosity can be inhibited, learning constrained, by a hostile or threatening environment. The learner, as with the infant, places herself in the hands of the Other, reliant on her experience, competence and good intent: the only ethical and humane response to such a situation of responsibility must be an attitude of 'care' (the German *Sorge*) on the part of the teacher.

And yet the teacher is not the first, nor the last, but rather takes her place within a chain of influences, while simultaneously allowing herself to be touched by the encounter with the student.

Dialogue

We are all each others' teachers.

> Through dialogue, the teacher-of-the-students and the students-of-the-teacher cease to exist and a new term emerges: teacher-student with students-teachers. The teacher is no longer merely the one who teaches, but one who is himself taught in the dialogue with the students, who in their turn while being taught also teach. They become jointly responsible for a process in which all grow. (Freire, 1972: 53)

Paulo Freire's dialogic model of teaching is particularly relevant to the field of psychotherapy training in that it rejects the notion that the teacher should be accorded a privileged status as the possessor of superior knowledge or the one who imparts wisdom. The dialogic teacher is a participant in an intersubjective process; she is one who 'lets learn' and learns.

The parties to this sort of learning/teaching dialogue partake of a lived, sensational, experience of the whole being. In this way, dialogue entails reciprocity, mutuality, not necessarily equality or evenness, but rather a to-ing and fro-ing – one opens oneself, receives and is responded to:

> Response is the act of turning to the other and confirming him as a Thou and not using him as an It. Men may turn toward or away from the other, that is, respond or refuse or fail to respond. True response can

45

come only with full responsibility for the other who is entrusted to me. Man's responsibility is a response to the divine call. (Buber, cited in Goldenberg and Isaacson, 1996: 126)

Implicit in that openness and receptivity is a willingness to allow for vulnerability on the part of my self and the Other.

The dialogical principle teaches us a number of things: first of all, we are fundamentally and irretrievably dialogic, conversational creatures whose lives are created in and through conversations and sustained or transformed in and through conversations. We learn that the very processes of our mind – including how we think, how we reason, how we know, how we solve problems, and so forth – are best grasped by examining the conversations in the social worlds we inhabit, which we appropriate and use. We learn that the qualities of our personality and identity are likewise constituted conversationally and sustained through our dialogues and various others. (Sampson, 1993: 108, cited in Gordon, 1999: 70–71)

Conversation with all its spoken and unspoken dimensions is a very subtle craft. As a therapist I attempt to have a particular sort of conversation, curiously one where I may speak very little. And as a teacher of psychotherapy I am attempting to assist in the development of that capacity to be-with another person, while also attempting to demonstrate such an attitude myself.

Within the learning context there is a conversational style often mistaken for dialogue; what happens is what could be described as a partial turning towards the Other. This type of conversation overlays the internal 'Oh yeah, that prompts me to say such and such,' or 'This comes to mind.' There is exchange and a visible rhythm, but the parties are essentially bounded by their own concerns, using each other as audience, and remain isolated and preoccupied by their own separate thoughts and sensations. Such an exchange may be exhilarating and stimulating and thus rewarding in itself; in fact, an awareness that anything more may be possible is often lacking.

But the dialogic principle provides a fundamental underpinning to one's engagement with the world as a whole; it is a way of involving and implicating oneself. There is potentially an 'everydayness' about it; it is not a way of being reserved for particular circumstances.

> The signs of address are not something extraordinary, something that steps out of the order of things, they are just what goes on in any case, nothing is added by the address. The waves of the ether roar on always, but for most of the time we have turned off our receivers. (Goldenberg and Isaacson, 1996: 126)

Having said that, particular circumstances may foster and facilitate dialogue more than others. Dialogue is primarily about the quality of the receptivity and willingness between people, not about the topic of conversation. The lack of such an atmosphere is something one doesn't necessarily notice in the moment. Its absence can emerge as a sour aftertaste: 'Yeuch – what was he actually saying?' or ... 'She misunderstood me', or ... 'He just talked over me', or ... 'I've come away feeling bad.'

H: For example: I just had a conversation. I didn't find it satisfying. I experienced all sorts of uncomfortable sensations, which I understood as feeling/being patronized, talked 'to', rather than 'with'; being dictated to, my requests being overruled, the locus of control being taken away from me. And the person I was speaking with experienced me as being 'resistant'. As it happens that person had set out, seemingly with the best of intentions, to 'help' me, and in some sort of concrete way, he did. I gained information I hadn't had and I started thinking about the undertaking more fully, while at the same time beginning to recognize all my hesitations. So, yes, it was a useful meeting, but I realized during the conversation: 'This could be different,' 'This could feel different', 'This could be done differently.' And ... afterwards, 'I could have been different in the exchange.' What came to mind was an earlier conversation of a similar nature that had taken place with another person, which achieved that different tone, atmosphere, that felt facilitative, helpful, where I felt able to acknowledge that someone had some knowledge I didn't have, while not feeling diminished by that fact, or irritated, or hurt by their manner.

The two conversations described above highlight two styles of conversation within a learning context: the first indicates the status of my interlocutor as someone who 'knows', and who sets the agenda and direction for the interaction; the second demonstrates that my agenda as a learner was respected – 'help' was given according to my needs, rather than the needs of the 'teacher'. Clearly teachers have a responsibility for setting the agenda in an overall sense, but within that given context, it is the learning of the student that should prescribe the content of the interaction.

In contrast, dialogue, although never complete, often leaves a clean, satisfied feeling.

M: It's so interesting that sometimes you need to think about it afterwards, that it cannot be evident in the now, but there is something that is left over ...

> It is only retrospectively, when I have withdrawn from
> the dialogue and am recalling it that I am able to
> reintegrate it into my life and make of it an episode in
> my private history ... (Merleau-Ponty, 1962: 354)

And yet, for some, the 'nakedness' of being 'met' or 'seen' leads to a degree of exposure which is to be avoided at all costs. The therapeutic encounter holds the potential for intimacy which is recognized and respected by some, recognized and guarded against by others. This is a controversial area within therapeutic circles. It was Freud himself who discovered the potential of the 'real relationship'. Adam Phillips suggests we should learn a capacity for 'impersonal intimacy' (Phillips, 2002). There is a penetrating aspect to dialogue which means that as well as engaging with the Other I am forced to engage with myself; which leads to the question of whether I have the courage to listen and engage in such an internal dialogue.

Dialogue, with its implicit openness, allows for all forms of real engagement, including confrontation with difficult aspects of reality, and the potential for conflict between people. In any real engagement there must be room for disagreement and conflict.

H: There is such a range of attitudes towards conflict, and there's something about the tendency to be wounded so easily, or how easily old wounds are tapped into. This is both a very personal and a very contextual topic. Attitudes towards conflict, including definitions of what conflict is, are set out at a national and ethnic level, as well as more intimately – the culture of my household, neighbourhood, my generation. We're again attempting to communicate across styles of language. I feel like a bit of an innocent at times; I want to ask the question: 'What's wrong with disagreeing?'

M: There's nothing 'wrong' with it, but at the same time it clearly raises anxiety levels and one then becomes less able to think or to formulate in a careful way or in a way that can be heard or whatever, and the thing goes wrong, the communication becomes damaging. Disagreeing is something very hard to do, it's so impossible to avoid pain; whatever you do, however you disagree, there's going to be some pain in it. People say: 'If I criticize your work I'm not criticizing you as a person', but clearly that is how it is perceived more often than not. There's such scope in a training endeavour as deeply personal as this for a student to feel profoundly damaged by criticism, however 'appropriate', of academic or clinical work, into which she has poured what feels like her deepest and most private self.

H: There's such thinly disguised fragility. But I think it's very interesting from a developmental point of view; when you say: '... however you disagree, there's going to be some pain in it' – how and why is that so? The problem is that we seem to find it so difficult to be disagreed with; we want consensus; there often seems to be something odd or uncomfortable about having a singular view. Being disagreed with seems to imply: 'You're wrong; I don't value what you're saying; I'm better than you; I'm smarter than you.' What underlies the difficulty with disagreement is the intensity of all the implied or inferred messages. Ultimately, perhaps, it's annihilation that we fear.

But what I would like to consider is: what if there was nothing wrong with being disagreed with, if we didn't have to have consensus, if there was nothing odd or uncomfortable about having a singular view, if being disagreed with didn't have all these hurtful, diminishing connotations? It's this big question about sameness and difference – 'differing' with me implies you and I are different, there is a chasm between us, but as Buber says:

> ... one can enter into relation only with a being that has
> been set at a distance, more precisely, has become an
> independent opposite. (Buber, cited in Goldenberg and
> Isaacson, 1996: 122)

So how did we come to be so frightened? I guess I would want
to add that ideally what we, as therapists and as teachers, attempt
to embody is a sense of not being quite so frightened, or at least
demonstrating our attempt to grapple with that fear. I think fear
begets fear, and steadfastness begets a safer environment. Its all a
part of the 'cradling', or at least one would hope so.

M: But think how frightened we can be. We know how the
experience of feeling 'different' can paralyse and inhibit, that it
often takes great courage to dare to stand against what appears to
be either a majority view or a strongly held conviction. But I
agree that to learn to tolerate disagreement is a key developmental 'good'. MacMurray (1961: 88–9) talks about how
necessary it is for the child to experience the 'rhythm of
withdrawal and return', and the experience of disagreement can
be one of those moments when we feel the relationship with the
Other has broken down, and we're thrown into irrationality.

H: But I think the opposite is also true. My willingness right this
moment to disagree with you is an honouring and respect of you
as a person, and a demonstration of the trust in our relationship
and the intent in our communication. I am 'showing' myself to
you rather than shying away from potential conflict. But the
wounds we all carry are so easy to tap into, be it in the student,
the teacher, or even the institution. If I am in dialogue then my
partners are not adversaries. I think the task of teaching demands
a kind of resilience, which is to do with resisting the temptation
of self-protectiveness, and being able to differentiate between the

different elements of the communication; to 'listen' and to 'hear', a challenge which may show itself more uncomfortably in the classroom than the consulting room. I would have thought that if we are attempting anything we should be seeking to develop those sorts of very delicate skills to apply in many situations; whereby noticing, wondering, questioning and being open to try and consider and understand might potentially become a way of going about your business, you know, your 'daily business'.

How We Learn

Before one can teach one must give thought to what it is to learn, a process we have all been engaged with since birth.

An exponential leap forward has occurred within the last twenty to thirty years in our understanding of how infants develop and learn, for example through the work of researchers such as Daniel Stern (1985) and, more recently, Allen Schore (1994). Stern (1985: 6) proposes that, in and through interpersonal processes, 'language and self-reflection ... transform or even create senses of the self that would come into existence at the very moment they become the subject matter of self-reflection'. Schore's seminal work shows how 'the early social environment, mediated by the primary caregiver, directly influences the evolution of structures in the brain that are responsible for the future social-emotional development of the child' (Schore,1994: 62). Adult learners, particularly those involved in the interpersonal and intersubjective learning environment of psychotherapy training, participate in similar processes – are engaged in growing new selves.

Chilton Pearce highlights the cyclical rhythm of learning, reminding us that it is an organic process to be facilitated in a manner that goes hand in hand with our natural tendencies:

... human beings are designed to grow in intelligence by learning about, and gaining ability to interact with, one source of energy, possibility, and security after another. The sequence is from early concrete matrices to ever more abstract ones, that is, from the matrix of our given life substance to the matrix of pure creative thought. Each matrix shift propels us into another set of unknown, unpredictable experiences, which is the way intelligence grows. Each matrix shift is both a kind of birth because we move into greater possibilities and a kind of death because the old matrix must be given up in order to move into the new. (Pearce, 1977: 16–17)

It is essential to work with the incremental nature of learning when undertaking the teaching/learning of psychotherapy. The learning involved in becoming a psychotherapist highlights the birth/death metaphor referred to by Chilton Pearce – a learning which is often so personally challenging.

Further, all our interactions in the name of education can take place only within an adequate holding framework – a 'system of reliable counterpoint – regulated by the laws of the different forms of relating – of giving and withholding oneself, intimacy and distance' (Buber, 1947: 112–13) which provides a regular rhythm of supports, boundaries, checks and balances for both teacher and learner.

The Learning

Learning is not the accumulation of scraps of knowledge. It is a growth, where every act of knowledge develops the learner, thus making him capable of constituting ever more and more complex objectivities – and the object

53

growth in complexity parallels the subjective growth in capacity. (Lauer, cited in May, 1969: 223)

Therapy training is, like the therapeutic process itself, somewhat difficult to 'explain'; like so many of life's experiences it is not something that can be adequately spoken of in the abstract. We often use phrases such as 'personal and professional' to indicate that in the therapy business the personal and professional are intricately and inextricably intertwined.

M: Which is a polite way of saying that psychotherapy trainees very often have to dig down deep within themselves to find the means to grow through their own woundedness. It may seem that an 'academic' training is likely to privilege the intellectual over the experiential, yet my experience of 'academic supervision' (as an example) has so often involved being present to students' desperately courageous struggles with personal issues, in order to learn, and to articulate that learning on the page. So many essays and dissertations are truly written in 'blood, sweat and tears'.

> Wisdom is often born in the shadows, frequently more present in the darkness than in the light. The stadium lights of knowledge that seek to eliminate natural cycles of night and day, death and rebirth, sorrow and joy do not cast shadows – they provide only the steady glare of illumination. We must move into darker places if we are to find the wisdom we so desperately need. We rarely go there willingly, though every life contains its own cycles of grief and celebration. To meet wisdom in these dark places we must be willing and able to hold all of what life gives us, to exclude nothing of ourselves or the world, to tell ourselves the truth. Wisdom will stretch us far beyond where we thought we could or wanted to go. She

will show us what we cannot change or control, reveal
what is hard to know about ourselves and the world, and
tear at the illusions of what we think we know, until we
are surrounded by the vastness of the mystery. (Oriah
Mountain Dreamer, 1999: 41)

Students often approach the learning with a keenness, a
preparedness and a nervousness, around the anticipation of
developing capacities and acquiring 'knowledge'. What often
comes as a surprise is that the learning demands a willingness to
'lose' as well as to 'gain', to go into the unknown, to 'unlearn',
and learn afresh; the challenging of ways of being, the clarifi-
cation of values and attitudes, the encouragement of
ever-increasing self-knowledge, all intertwined with the developing capacity to sit with an Other.

> The therapeutic relationship is seen as a heightening of
> the constructive qualities which often exist in part in
> other relationships and an extension through time of
> qualities which in other relationships tend at best to be
> momentary. (Rogers, 1967: 134)

Teachers, too, usually approach the learning with an enthusiasm
and a nervousness, with questions like: 'Will I be able to facilitate
learning in an Other?'. What often comes as a surprise is the
personal learning that takes place, if once again the teacher can
allow herself to be taught. And perhaps a crucial aspect of what
is being taught and what is hopefully being learnt is a respect for
the unpredictability of the learning opportunities that present
themselves in all the dimensions of our lives. So once again:

> Through dialogue, the teacher-of-the-students and the
> students-of-the-teacher cease to exist and a new term

emerges: teacher-student with students-teachers. The teacher is no longer merely the one who teaches, but one who is himself taught in the dialogue with the students, who in their turn while being taught also teach. They become jointly responsible for a process in which all grow. (Freire, 1972: 53)

So You Are a Teacher ...?

The true teacher is ... the one who fosters genuine mutual contact and mutual trust, who experiences the other side of the relationship, and who helps his pupils realise, through the selection of the effective world, what it can mean to be a man. (Friedman, in Buber, 1947, 2002: xviii)

What then makes a talented and effective teacher? Teaching is often regarded as a vocation (a branch of the 'helping professions'), when it is not considered a 'career' path pursued out of desperation. As a vocation, teaching represents a form of engagement with the Other – an Other who is younger/knows less/would benefit from my experience/expertise/communication capacities. To be a teacher argues a commitment to the future, an investment of hope and energy in the ongoing-ness of the world. Never forget that the agenda of the teacher is always a (r)evolutionary one: therapy too is a (r)evolutionary activity, and we believe permeates beyond the consulting room, into the life and social network of both therapist and client, and further.

Yet the corollary must be considered alongside: in remaining with 'children' – the learners – do I somehow seek gratification through comparison with 'beginners', rather than taking the risk of measuring myself against the 'grown-ups'? In the field of professional training in psychotherapy, tutors are required also to be practitioners in order to ensure that teaching is firmly grounded in experience ... It is cynically said of teachers: 'Those who can, do, and those that can't, teach.' Psychotherapy is such a personally lived endeavour, it is vital that teachers 'do' as well as 'teach', in fact that the 'teaching' is a 'doing', or more accurately a 'being-with', which simultaneously is a 'modelling'.

So what does it mean to present myself as a teacher of psychotherapy? When standing in front of a class of trainees to what extent am I knowingly presenting myself as a model? And, if so, a model of what? In the arena of therapy training, how do I enact and embody my radical responsibility for the Other, for the trainee psychotherapist? What is that responsibility? We pose these questions and argue they are essential questions to be grappled with throughout one's career; ultimate answers may elude us.

> The teacher is ahead of his apprentices in this alone, that he has still far more to learn than they – he has to learn to let them learn. The teacher must be capable of being more teachable than the apprentices. The teacher is far less sure of his material than those who learn are of theirs. If the relation between the teacher and the learner is genuine, therefore, there is never a place in it for the authority of the know-it-all or the authoritative sway of the official.
> (Heidegger, 1977, cited in Gans and Redler, 2001: 79)

We place ourselves and our 'hierarchic' evaluations and judgements in the way of 'constant correction' (Buber, 1947) through the counter-evaluations and judgments of our students.

And so we call to mind our own positive models:

H: A teacher, who had the ability to facilitate discovery of my approach, which was other than his own. He demonstrated how to challenge, how not to be indoctrinating or pontificating. He showed that teaching can be having an awareness of potential, exerting the self-restraint not to squeeze, suffocate, or seek to make in one's own image, simply to 'cradle'. A therapist, who demonstrated what it is to remain steadfast and unflinching; to safeguard my sense of safety by virtue of his own resilience; to make those subtle judgements about tenderness and compassion and stubbornness and determination.

M: A teacher who impressed because of his radical determination to approach questions that he himself found problematic, wrestling with the difficulty in an open but not intrusive way. Another who sought, with humour and humility, to make transparent her own bias, her selectivity in regard to the ideas of others, in such a way as to allow students uncluttered access to the core of the writer's position. A supervisor who would not flinch from inferred commentary on her own part in guiding and managing sessions, and in maintaining or securing the frame.

From all of these have been absorbed a passion for learning, for something like 'truth' (which has within it something of the 'good'), a way of succeeding in 'standing forth' as an individual while not 'standing in the path of the learner'.

And so we aspire to embody some of what we know to be possible.

The Moment of Living a Teacher

Teaching includes a performative element: the individual who places herself in front of a group of students promises to convey knowledge and understanding to her audience, or to communicate something of her own learning or experience. Her audience would not be there, or she would not be thus employed, were it not that she claimed to have something that her audience either needed or wanted. Such communication involves qualities and skills, some of which pertain to the actor, some to the parent/mentor, some to the scholar or practitioner.

The teacher as performer must master the skills of holding the attention of her audience, must have skills of vocal delivery and of timing. She must tailor her material to fit within the given timescale. She must engage and enthuse her audience, so that they feel that they are being initiated into a field of knowledge and a particular kind of awareness that holds out a new vision of the world, in however small a degree. She must leave room for questioning, for alternative opinions, for assent, disagreement or resistance, so that her audience recognize themselves as engaged in dialogue, rather than being 'talked at'.

H: It can be childlike too. It can be fun. You can acknowledge you're having fun, even being playful. You know, when I give my definitions about what counselling or therapy is, there's one definition that seems to provoke the same response time and again, and I get a real kick out of that. It's a pretty crude definition:

> Counselling is an interpersonal influence process ... First
> counsellors enhance their perceived expertness,
> attractiveness, trustworthiness, and the client's
> involvement in counselling ... (Strong and Claiborn,
> 1982: 396)

Students are always aghast, to which I respond: 'Think about it, think about what's going on right now, and the effort to which I have gone so that we are having a nice time with each other. I want you to think that I have some idea of what I'm talking about, so that you feel safe and I'll feel respected and we can approach each other.' That's manipulation. It's hopefully not abuse, but it is manipulation. I guess that's the difference between teaching which embodies an I–Thou stance, and teaching of an I–It nature. Yes, there is a performance element, potentially where everyone is engaged, feels involved and respected. The alternative is that I as teacher actually want the learners to remain passive, so I can pontificate, and not be challenged, in fact, be careful not to leave any space for that.

M: And yet that is not a good performance, because a good teaching performance has the pedagogic aim of eliciting a real response, a thinking response, rather than just unthinking and facile applause. So it is indeed a game with a manipulative element. That speaks to the complexity of the interaction: I want this to be enjoyable; I want this to be fun, engrossing, and this is how I'm going to manage it. There are two factors operating, working together for the outcome of the learning.

H: So we can come to a win-win situation: I can feel good and the students can feel good and we can enjoy that in each other. But once again, I think that demands an openness, a non-defensive attitude.

M: It does, but it also quite cleverly uses the defences or awareness of the defences of the others, that's the manipulation, you encourage the dropping of the defences; that can be done.

H: A dialogical style actually fosters a sense in students that they are an essential part of the learning; they're being respected, they have a responsibility – the learning itself is more of a collabo-rative effort. What comes to mind is that a defended stance on the part of the teacher is often spotted, and sets off a nervousness and a need to test on the part of students. It can feel like they're out to get you. So that self-protectiveness works against you. I guess that comes back to the question of what we are modelling. Where students legitimately feel disillusioned is when they don't see that in the teaching: 'Do as I say, not as I do.'

M: They see defensiveness in action, dissonant with the words, they implicitly feel diminished into an It – 'the students'. But that brings to mind the advantage in having a group of people to teach who have different ideas, approaches, and capabilities in teaching, but who in sum manifest a 'good-enough' capacity for dialogue, somehow managing to work and be together. This involves staying with what it means to be different and to accept shortcomings in the institution – the people who, as a group, form the learning community.

H: We should make the collaborative nature of the teaching/learning clear from the beginning, we should say outright: 'We're going to teach each other'; its so easy to get fixed into the role of teacher or student, and to define the roles as mutually exclusive.

M: Separated and alienated from each other.

Much of what we have just spoken about applies to the therapeutic encounter as much as the teacher/learner situation.

While as therapist I may reject the 'expert' model, and make no claim to 'know', as teacher I may be presenting myself as a bearer of intellectual and theoretical information. But accumulated knowledge or experience is not necessarily the only or the foremost prerequisite of qualities in the prospective teacher; some of the best university tutors are those who are recently graduated, and thus retain a freshness and an enthusiasm for the subject and an openness to their own continuing learning about it as much as a depth of knowledge or experience. A certain lack of confidence in one's worthiness as a 'teacher' is an asset rather than a liability, since it sharpens the learning faculties!

The best teachers are those who have a commitment to their own learning, and it is a truism that the best way to learn one's subject from the inside is to teach it. The discipline involved in both marshalling the accumulation of knowledge or learning in a field in order to offer an overview or a précis of it, and of communicating this to a group of learners is clearly an exercise that itself brings significant learning through the familiarization process.

The learning agenda of the teacher is also a consideration. The question that arises here is: 'What am I here to learn from this activity and from this person/these people?'.

M: I have found that the most significant interactions for me in a training context are those in which my sense of satisfaction relates to what I believe I have learnt about how to be. Sometimes this relates to a 'weak', diffuse sense of 'this has been an interesting experience'. Less often, but more meaningful, are those occasions when I know that I have been privileged to learn something for myself, that being-together with another, or with a particular group has resulted in a sense of communion which is enhancing to me, the feeling of having been 'given' something from out of the 'togetherness' that restores or repairs something in me. This feels like 'transferable' learning that will enable me in some way in another situation.

H: Indeed ... 'we are all each other's teachers' ...

M: I am so aware of the immeasurable privilege of witnessing so much profound learning; we do not adequately acknowledge and honour the full-hearted courage, the sheer grit and dogged determination to continue, that characterizes so many students. Quite often I feel that I hitch a ride on the learning of the students ...

Living Learning

Freire proposes a 'problem-posing education', based on creativity, which 'stimulates true reflection and action upon reality, thereby responding to the vocation of men as beings who are authentic only when engaged in inquiry and creative transformation' (Freire, 1972: 56), and sees dialogue as an existential necessity: 'the encounter between men, mediated by the world, in order to name the world . . . If it is in speaking their word that men transform the world by naming it, dialogue imposes itself as the way in which men achieve significance as men' (p. 61).

We would wholeheartedly agree with Freire that such a model of teaching cannot exist in the absence of 'a profound love for the world and for men . . . without humility, without an intense faith in man, faith in his power to make and remake, to create and recreate, faith in his vocation to be more fully human'. Given these, 'dialogue becomes a horizontal relationship of which mutual trust between the participants is a logical consequence' (p. 64). Further, the teacher is committed to a sense of hope, 'rooted in humanity's incompleteness, from which we move out in constant search – a search which can be carried out only in communion with other men' (*loc. cit.*). Finally, he concludes,

> . . . dialogue cannot exist unless it involves critical
> thinking – thinking which discerns an indivisible
> solidarity between the world and men admitting of no
> dichotomy between them – thinking which does not
> separate itself from action, but constantly immerses itself
> in temporality without fear of the risks involved. (p. 65)

The everydayness of dialogue is often not appreciated. The potential for dialogue comes into all our teaching/learning encounters – in and out of the classroom. To attempt to embody the dialogic principle is not like donning a coat that you can take off; it is a way of being which comes with you into that space where you present yourself as the facilitator of learning; it is an attitude which informs the teaching/learning/teaching process.

> The world ... has its influence as nature and as society on the child. He is educated by the elements, by air and light and the life of plants and animals, and he is educated by relationships. The true educator represents both; but he must be to the child as one of the elements. (Buber, 1947: 107)

But, '... only one element amidst the fullness of life, only one single existence in the midst of all the tremendous inrush of reality on the [learner]' (*ibid*: 126). A light touch is required: 'this almost imperceptible, most delicate approach, the raising of a finger, perhaps, or a questioning glance', 'the important influence ... of criticism and instruction' should be used sparingly and with respect for the autonomy of the learner. Buber cautions against 'interference' on the part of the teacher, which 'divides the soul in his care into an obedient and a rebellious part' (*ibid.* p. 107), when what works is the integrating force proceeding from the personal integrity of the teacher.

We recognize, along with Buber, the 'light touch' implicit in the 'cradling', the vital backdrop of the learner's confidence and trust in the teacher, which we argue is (must be, in fact) fostered by the willingness of the teacher to shoulder responsibility for the teacher/learner relationship in a way analogous to the therapist/client relationship. In both, the relationship is simultaneously profoundly reciprocal, while remaining asymmetrical.

3
'Being-Together'

Perhaps the scriptwriter of the film *Being There*, one of the last films that Peter Sellers made, was a follower of the philosopher Martin Heidegger. German speakers tell us that 'Being-there' is an inadequate translation of the term 'Dasein'. We're told that the significance of the translation, including the hyphen, is the acknowledgement of the relational aspect of existence. When we speak of 'being-there' we're not simply talking about being, but being somewhere, in some particular social context, as a crucial element in the fact of one's being, one's existence.

The film highlighted in a very clever, satirical fashion, the extent to which we create each other; the extent to which we do not see or hear what 'is', but what we need or want, or are able, to see or hear; the degree to which we are not 'there', present with an Other, but are usually so consumed by our own preconceptions, assumed meanings, etc. that we do not even realize it is so. This blindness can be so powerful that the simple words of a gardener may be invested with strategic or metaphysical import and meaning.

To a great extent we exist within our own separate 'bubbles'. We establish our view of life and the world around us and apply many means to keep that view intact. As Heidegger suggests, we humans have the unique quality of being able to stand out of ourselves and notice that we are, that we exist in time and place.

'Dasein' is seen as a complex notion not adequately translatable, not simply because of the limitations of the English language, but because of the enormity of the concept, which borders on the mystical or the spiritual, hinting at the potential scope of being human – which is daunting, overwhelming and never fully actualized.

As psychotherapists we attempt to be-there, to be present; in fact we attempt to truly be-together-with another. No one describes the potentiality of this being-together more evocatively than the philosopher, teacher and theologian Martin Buber:

> When I was eleven years of age, spending the summer on my grandparents' estate, I used, as often as I could do it unobserved, to steal into the stable and gently stroke the neck of my darling, a broad dapple-grey horse. It was not a casual delight but a great, certainly friendly, but also deeply stirring happening. If I am to explain it now, beginning from the still very fresh memory of my hand, I must say that what I experienced in touch with the animal was the Other, the immense otherness of the Other, which, however, did not remain strange like the otherness of the ox and the ram, but rather let me draw near and touch it. When I stroked the mighty mane, sometimes marvellously smooth-combed, at other times just as astonishingly wild, and felt the life beneath my hand, it was as though the element of vitality itself bordered on my skin, something that was not I, was certainly not akin to me, palpably the other, not just another, really the Other itself; and yet it let me approach, confided itself to me, placed itself elementally in the relation of *Thou* and *Thou* with me. The horse, even when I had not begun by pouring oats for him into the manger, very gently raised his massive head, ears

flicking, then snorted quietly, as a conspirator gives a signal meant to be recognisable only by his fellow-conspirator; and I was approved. But once – I do not know what came over the child, at any rate it was child-like enough – it struck me about the stroking, what fun it gave me, and suddenly I became conscious of my hand. The game went on as before, but something had changed, it was no longer the same thing. And the next day, after giving him a rich feed, when I stroked my friend's head he did not raise his head. A few years later, when I thought back to the incident, I no longer supposed that the animal had noticed my defection. But at the time I considered myself judged. (Buber 1965: 22, 23)

This moving recollection illustrates the paradoxical nature of relation; so powerful while terribly delicate and fragile – a split-second lapse having profound repercussions. It highlights the preciousness, and precariousness of the possibilities of encounter with an Other.

The story also indicates the temporality in which relation is situated: such quality of attention wanes, and the moment – the possibility of the I–Thou meeting – evaporates. Also of note is the child's sense of being judged, which suggests his heightened sense of responsibility for the possibility of relation, and the finality of the judgement – there is no going back. Lastly, there is a warning in the story for therapists: as soon as one becomes self-conscious, particularly of one's enjoyment of the moment, and of the meeting, then the moment, and the meeting, are gone, and a repetition can, and arguably should, never be sought or found again.

Some of us have personal experience of the intensity and intimacy which Buber alludes to in this tale, and in much of his writing, but few of us are as awake as he to the possibility of such intimate meeting. Buber challenges us to discover within ourselves the capacity for this quality of meeting, which some might describe as a 'mystic' experience.

His notion of 'that state of shared possibility – the Between' (Goldenberg and Isaacson, 1996: 123) refers to a degree of reciprocal engagement rarely realized by many, including many therapists, but it could be argued that it is precisely at these rare moments of genuine, full, uncalculated 'being to being' meeting that therapy, or, for that matter, teaching/learning takes place.

H: In discussion with a client, as our therapeutic relationship was ending, she commented that it was her experience that my eyes welled up, when she got choked up – that our physiological processes mirrored each other, seemingly involuntarily; we met 'soul to soul'. That was my sense as well. I was moved, gratified, and oh-so-conscious of the mystery. One cannot 'will' this sort of meeting; one can only be intently open to the possibility.

M: Similarly ... my/our own experience of such moments, for example, with a group of students at the end of an intensive course, or, as recently for me, at what may have been an occasion of premature termination of the 'teacher/learner' relationship. The intensity derived from the 'pain' of the moment which was nevertheless allied to the 'gain' we all acknowledged as existing (mutually) in our relationship to this point.

R. D. Laing describes a meeting with a particular client as an illustration of what he calls 'rapport', and says:

> ... as I'm listening to her I'm hanging on every word
> she's saying, and as I'm talking she's hanging on every
> word I'm saying. There's a certain pace to my pauses and
> talk mirrored very vividly in her eye movements, in her

blinking, in her mouth movements, in the most intimate muscle movements of her forehead and face; her face and my voice are now together, and then the very moment when I say 'ah', she flicks her tongue 'ah'. We were so much together, resonating in response to her story, at that moment I emitted a sound 'ah' and her physiological system inducted her to put her tongue out 'ah' – that is what I mean by 'rapport'. (Laing, 1976b)

Medard Boss, founder of Daseinsanalysis, speaks of the 'being-together' of the therapist/client meeting, and reminds us that it was Freud himself who first stressed the physician–patient relationship as the genuine basis of all forms of treatment: 'the being-together of physician and patient is where the treatment actually takes place ...' (Boss, 1979: 257–8)

It is the nature and quality of that 'being-together', that 'being-with-another', in both the therapeutic encounter and in the meeting of the teacher/learner grouping, which is central to our thought and enquiry in this writing.

Much of what takes place within therapy is precisely this struggle to be-with-an-Other, to 'be-together', a struggle for both client and therapist. Each comes with different expectations of the other and themselves, and there is an allocation (implicitly, or explicitly) of different tasks. For instance, my task as therapist may be to attempt to enter into the world of my client; to acknowledge my client as 'Other', while recognizing we are both 'one of the others'.

If this is my goal, then I, as therapist, have to take a stance that allows for sameness and difference. In fact, this openness to a rhythmic shifting between meeting and divergence is the only way I can really be in relation, but this is no mean feat, and is often the issue throughout the therapeutic relationship.

How often, in order to 'seemingly' be-with my client, do I

deny his/her otherness from me? To what extent does acknowledging – the ways in which s/he presents me with difference,
with the unfamiliar – rock my sense of me? By engaging with the
otherness of the Other, I am simultaneously confronted with my
otherness from the Other. I may recognize the Other as 'not-me',
while at the same time the otherness of the Other throws light on
what 'is' me; and, perhaps more uncomfortably, raises questions
about what is me. Here we come to the feature of the Other as
not simply not me, but also different from me. Emmanuel
Levinas (1962), with his terminology of 'same' and 'Other', is
perhaps the boldest in confronting this issue. In recognizing and
allowing the Other to be other, I have to grapple with the impact
of his otherness on my sense of me. If he is other than me, what
does that say about me? In other words, truly facing the Other,
also leads me to have to face myself.

Often students, even more dramatically than clients, lead me
to have to face myself, my anxiety, my self-doubt, my need for
the attention and adulation of an audience, my competitiveness.
On the other hand, the potential for a shared experience, or those
fleeting moments of real connection, when recognition and
learning for teacher and learners hover almost palpably in the air
are the embodiment of 'being-together'. Our 'being-together' as
teacher/learners/teachers is an ongoing challenge for all parties.

H: Which brings me back to our collaboration and reactions to
it. You and I 'dialogue', we are in dialogue. That is a fundamental
theme of this book and is embodied in the writing of the book,
and I think this process replicates the teaching process and the
therapeutic process. And yet, one of our ex-students commented:
'I hear you are writing a book, how are you doing it . . . because
of your different approaches?'. Such comments puzzle me. I'm
left wondering: does that mean that people walk away from each
other? That countries walk away from each other, that people in

families who are in different positions in relation to each other, are they all meant to walk away from each other? The object of the exercise (and this is where I see a distinction between what people often describe as empathy and what I envisage) is being-with or being-together, which is precisely about trying – often not succeeding, but trying nonetheless – to make the leap to another vision, and about recognizing that we all have different visions.

M: To encompass another vision within my scheme of things, within myself, alongside my own, and to allow the two to impact on each other and bring something new out of that ...

H: And being able to 'hear'. That's why I always say empathy involves imagination. Fitting into shoes that fit is no huge accomplishment, it's about fitting in shoes that don't fit. It's the great difficulty people have with issues of sameness and difference. If you're so desperately searching out the 'sameness' in someone else to hold onto and are going to disregard all the bits that aren't the same, you've diminished that other person, while taking what I can only describe as a frightened position.

Again I'm noticing that, as the book is developing, our references are generally coming from different places; your style of writing is sometimes very different to mine. I notice that this is not my natural style, and I notice my sensations. It can be uncomfortable sometimes and I find myself taking a little gulp. I have to make a little effort – big deal. Because something doesn't instantly click do I just turn away from it?

M: I find that I tend to just try to sit with any possible feelings of difference, to wait to decide what I need to bring up for discussion ...

71

H: No matter what approach I may be using it is always about trying to see the wood for the trees, to get to the pain or the need or the quest, to wonder: 'What is that person trying to say?'. Certainly when we talk about working with so-called psychosis then there is an enormous amount of disentangling to do. Yet we consider that possible, so why is it not possible for people whose so-called ideology might be a bit different to have some respect and also to see that theory is not the truth, theory is just theory?

M: It's a way of talking about something.

H: It's a form of language. In essence, what's being suggested is that the Tower of Babel reigns. 'That's it, finished – we can't get beyond the "I".' I hear that as a sad, defeatist position.

The state of the world demonstrates the concrete urgency of the need to address the challenge of the Other. The power and danger of 'competing truth claims', as described by the French philosopher Paul Ricoeur (1991), has been all too starkly demonstrated, leading to cycles of political and physical dominance and persecution, destruction of peoples and cultures, and of the core of humanity.

The consulting room and the training process have an invaluable and timely part to play in the open engagement of Other to Other. We consider the interface between therapy and the outside world more fully in Chapters 4 and 7; for the moment, let it suffice to say that psychotherapy and therapy training do not exist in a vacuum. Just as practitioners must remain mindful of the potential harmful repercussions of the therapeutic meeting on the social context of its participants, its potentiality for the development of deepening modes of communication and meeting between peoples beyond the boundaries of the therapeutic setting cannot be overstated. Laing sets out the poetry and full magnitude of the undertaking:

> ... really to be with another person in a completely open-
> hearted, unguarded way, where one is not on one's own
> part or somehow or other, cancelling or changing or
> altering or modifying who that other person is to suit one's
> own good ... co-presence, being actually present to each
> other without reservation is a precondition of something
> that one might call communion which I think is the
> perfection of how we're ordinarily meant to be together –
> that's the only peace that's possible. (Laing, 1976)

Therapeutic practice imbued with existential ideas is based on the recognition of 'the intersubjective' – of the impact I have on the Other, and the Other's impact on me. As Spinelli writes:

> People tend to like and approve of a philosophy – and a
> therapeutic approach – which promotes freedom, choice
> and responsibility – so long as its more painful and
> complex co-constitutional implications are not given their
> necessary exposure, and so long as they can continue to
> adopt a stance of subjective exclusivity. Too often, for
> instance, the assumption of responsibility, while possibly
> painful, is acknowledged on the false ground that it refers
> only to subjective – rather than intersubjective –
> experience. In this way, the 'other's' experiential
> responsibility becomes a matter for the 'other' alone to
> deal with, and does not implicate the being with whom
> the 'other' is in relation. Such a stance promotes a
> separatist orientation towards being which is clearly at
> odds with crucial insights gleaned from existential
> phenomenology. (1996: 23–4)

... 'at odds' no doubt with much existential writing, most dramatically the work of Emmanual Levinas, who initiated a revolution when he spoke of our radical responsibility for the Other:

> I am for the Other whether the Other is for me or not;
> his responsibility for me is, so to speak, his problem,
> and whether or not he 'handles' that problem does not
> in the least affect my being-for-him (as far as my being-
> for-the Other includes respect for the Other's autonomy,
> which in its turn includes my consent not to blackmail
> the Other into being-for-me, nor interfere in any other
> way in the Other's freedom). Whatever else 'I-for-you'
> may contain, it does not contain a demand to be repaid,
> mirrored or 'balanced out' in the 'you-for-me'. My
> relation to the other is not reversible; if it happens
> to be reciprocated, the reciprocation is but an accident
> from the point of view of my being-for. (Bauman,
> 1993: 50)

Meeting

Yet meeting, while not necessarily implying balance or equality, does demand a movement 'towards' by both parties, an openness to the exchange. Buber speaks of an 'I–Thou stance'; quite simply, the task is how to cultivate an openness to the moment, to moments of unmediated contact with existence.

The work of Buber and Boss in particular informs the idea of the therapeutic 'meeting', which takes place between persons – one wholly embodied being together with an other. While we all have the capacity for such meeting, bringing ourselves fully towards the Other is the greatest human challenge. It is a given of existence that we are in relation, yet 'how to be in relation' remains a question central to the therapeutic endeavour.

H: I had just finished running a workshop, and there was a great deal of food left over. I was to travel on foot to meet a relative, so I just bundled up a bunch of cookies. I was walking down the street when I noticed someone on the street doing what from the distance looked like a weird dance, and as I'm walking, I'm trying to work out what he was doing. As I get close I see that he is near a rubbish bin, and he is actually trying to clean an apple, to shake it clean. I notice it as I'm walking and I'm actually past him already and then it just occurred to me . . .

I turned and said: 'Would you like some cookies?'. He said, 'I would love some cookies.' I walked back and handed him the cookies.

That was it; the exchange took place. I said, 'You have got to unpack them carefully because they are going to fall all over the place.'

He was stunned and just sort of waved after me, and then shouted, 'Thanks!'.

It was just a blissful moment. We didn't have to intrude on each other, no big expectations of each other – complete strangers – just fortuitous and perfect for both of us . . . I thought: 'Isn't that neat that I had those cookies at that moment.' . . . fabulous; it was simple, straight, clean.

M: Something standing out of the landscape of the day.

H: And good for the soul, 'the spirit':

> Spirit is not in the I, but between the I and Thou. It is not like the blood that circulates in you, but like the air in which you breathe. Man lives in the spirit if he is able to respond to his Thou. He is able to if he enters into

75

relation with his whole being. Only by virtue of his power to enter into relation is he able to live in the spirit. (Buber, cited in Goldenberg and Isaacson, 1996: 123)

Presence

Presence is not to be confused with a sentimental attitude toward the patient but depends firmly and consistently on how the therapist conceives of human beings. It is found in therapists of various schools and differing beliefs – differing, that is, on anything except one central issue – their assumptions about whether the human being is an object to be analyzed or a being to be understood. Any therapist is existential to the extent that, with all his technical training and his knowledge of transference and dynamisms, he is still able to relate to the patient as 'one existence communicating with another', to use Binswanger's phrase. In my own experience Freda Fromm-Reichmann particularly had this power in a given therapeutic hour; she used to say, 'The patient needs an experience, not an explanation.' (May, 1969: 81)

When there is meeting (encounter), what is between the I and Thou is a shared possibility beyond the singular. Wood describes Buber as having 'moved into a position which undercuts the subject-object dichotomy'...

Buber introduced the notion of an ontologically prior relation of Presence, binding subject and object together in an identity-in-difference which he termed the I-Thou relation and which constitutes the region of what he calls the Between. (Wood, 1969: 41)

'Meeting' between persons takes place when one is open, available, and receptive to that possibility. One needs to be 'present' in order for 'meeting' to become an actuality. We would suggest that essentially what the therapist is offering is her 'presence'. At its best, my meeting with the client encapsulates a profound openness towards what shows itself in our encounter, while at the same time everything I have ever experienced, learnt, been taught, imagined . . . is a resource to be called upon.

M: Your remark about the two kinds of conversations . . . yes.

H: Yes, sometimes I have that sense, an aftertaste, that my partner in conversation actually wasn't present. Irrespective of the topic (it can be anything from exchanging recipes to discussing the state of the world) I can come away with a satisfied feeling, or not. That's where it comes back to the centrality of attitude, some sort of shared attitude . . . I have a friend I have spoken to once a week for the past fourteen years; we go to some effort to find a little time slot; and having done that, on this occasion, as it turned out, I was not actually in a very good frame of mind, and I knew that I needed to use the time when we had agreed to speak instead to rest. I phoned my friend and told her. I was sad and disappointed for myself, but also didn't want to cause upset, and I could hear in her voice that it was fine and came away feeling sort of clean. I think it's about a quality of her actually hearing me, believing me, while also being concerned about my welfare. We're not talking about her being understanding.

Once again true dialogue is not about trying to get my point across, but about demonstrating my interest in the Other. When we're being quiet with clients, that can be felt as withholding, or it can be felt as being completely immersed in them. It's about managing to convey my interest in somebody else; that my interest goes beyond self-interest. It is being in relation, rather

77

than subject/object; the other is not just an audience to receive my pontificating.

M: Even if the meeting is only in a shared joke or something, and not necessarily a great meeting of minds, a synthesis of something or other, but a shared flash of humour ... or a sense of irony ...

H: And that's the real connection, and that's often when you go beyond ... that is the human to human. I was thinking you often have those sorts of meetings with strangers ...

M: For me there is a going beyond the constraints of the relationship. In teaching those are the moments of connection between teacher and students which actually establish you in a person-to-person relationship, forget the teacher, the student, the evaluation, forget all of that, you just meet in a moment. As in the Buber story, it is a kind of meeting and whatever it means or whatever it doesn't mean is beside the point, the meeting is the meeting, and as soon as it is noticed, it disappears.

H: I would say, as soon as you noticed it, it is finished and you have stepped out of it.

The being-together of client and therapist includes a determination on both parts – a shared sense of 'not giving up'. In other words, the therapeutic process is a shared venture, and both parties must be committed. In fact while the therapeutic endeavour is portrayed as the journey of the client, that client's journey impinges on the therapist's. If I, as therapist, am truly to engage with the otherness of my client, in his/her particularity – truly to attempt to allow my own understanding of existence to be challenged and scrutinized – then it is I, the therapist, as much

78

as my client, who enters into an uncertain, unsettling, at times terrifying journey. Spinelli describes this as 'un-knowing' (1997), daring to unravel what I think I know. Involved is the recognition that being in relation means being touched, and perhaps being irrevocably altered by the encounter. As Levinas describes:

> The work thought radically is indeed a movement from the Same towards the other which never returns to the Same. To the myth of Ulysses returning to Ithaca, we would like to oppose the story of Abraham leaving his homeland forever for a still-unknown land and even forbidding his son to be brought back to his point of departure. (Levinas, 1974: 191)

On the Other Hand ...

The recognition of the full potentiality of the therapeutic meeting for both participants is something that is guarded against by many within the profession.

The language of psychoanalysis does not take kindly to discussion of 'being-together'. The twin classical concepts of 'transference/countertransference' have encouraged a false dichotomy between the 'transference relationship' and the 'real relationship' between therapist and client. The therapist's subjectivity becomes defined only in terms of the client, who therefore bears the burden of responsibility. The 'Other's' experiential responsibility becomes a matter for the 'other' alone to deal with, and does not implicate the being with whom the 'other' is in relation (Spinelli, 1996: 24).

The possibility of a person-to-person meeting in the analytic encounter has been overshadowed by the 'rule of abstinence' of 'classical' psychoanalysis. This injunction is based on the idea that to gratify the client's 'regressive' need for relationship is to offer false reassurance, to lose sight of more appropriate developmental goals. Yet, from Fairbairn and Winnicott onwards, psychoanalysts have been giving of themselves unstintingly in their interaction with clients. This capacity to be-with is described by Coltart:

> to sit it out with a patient, often for long periods,
> without any real precision as to where we are, relying on
> our regular tools and our faith in the process to carry us
> through the obfuscating darkness of resistance, and the
> sheer unconsciousness of the unconscious. (1992: 3)

She also claims that, in the quest for 'truth, and more importantly, authenticity, in our style of speech we must also master intuitive, unlaboured spontaneity' (*ibid.*, 142), finding that, to achieve this, we need 'a combination of unselfconscious self-forgetfulness and deep self-confidence' (Kennedy, 1998: 129).

Only relatively recently have psychoanalytic theorists (e.g. Bollas, 1987; Kennedy, 1998; Lomas, 1999, 2001; Schafer, 1976) begun to focus more particularly on the quality of the 'real' relationship facilitated by the therapist, beginning to conceptualize an intersubjective understanding of psychoanalytic psychotherapy, which proposes therapist and client as inter-related, interdependent, co-creating each other and the analytic experience – 'the third subject' – as they interact. However, Kennedy maintains:

> The analytic relationship, though an intimate one, is also
> a distorted one, where the subjectivities of analyst and
> patient are not the same or are not at the same level; the
> patient's world is to be examined in the open, while the
> analyst's is essentially private, or masked, except at a few
> contact points with the patient. (Kennedy, 1998: 65)

Such a distortion reflects the inequity in the relationship and provides an opportunity for the radical being-for-the-other of the therapist.

Kennedy also insists that the therapist's self-reflection be confined to 'the disciplined use of the analyst's countertransference' (*loc. cit.*), while, following Bion, others are more open to awareness of their own 'reveries, forms of mental activity that appear to be nothing more than narcissistic self-absorption, distractedness, compulsive rumination, daydreaming and the like' (Ogden, 1994: 94–5). '[O]ne may be listening for the way chains of meaning, narrative structures or "voices", criss-cross, intermix, fade, dissolve or occasionally cohere' (Kennedy, 1998: 68), for oneself as for the Other. Kennedy quotes Viederman who describes the position of many analysts of the 'old school' that '[t]o give theoretical status to the personal attributes and responses of the analyst ... generates concern that the definition of the analytic process will be clouded and its scientific status compromised' (Viederman, 1991: 459, cited in Kennedy, 1998: 122). Thus practitioners wrestle with notions of the 'neutrality' of the analytic encounter.

Peter Lomas offers a 'commonsense' account of what might be the elements of an attitude on the part of the therapist which promotes creative relationship. He speaks in favour of spontaneity on the part of the therapist, characterized as 'a quality of response that comes – insofar as this is possible – from the core of one's being rather than behaviour that has been rehearsed according to a plan, strategy or theory' (Lomas, 1999: 91).

What is developing through the writings of Kennedy, Ogden and others is an acknowledgement of the contribution of the analyst's or therapist's own being to the therapeutic project, and of her own deep emotional need both for the patient, and for the interaction as a means of addressing her own areas of suffering;

and that this is a 'vital and therapeutic element' of the relationship. Kennedy is not alone in pointing out that therapists need to listen to the patient's conscious and unconscious assessment of the therapist's private areas of pain and suffering.

Clearly, this blows the impassive 'blank screen' concept right out of the water, and resonates with the work of Robert Langs, who, in his communicative approach (e.g. Langs, 1982, 1988, 1992a, 1992b), actively focuses the work of the therapist on the client's 'unconscious' commentary ('feedback') on the interventions of the therapist.

Langs's communicative perspective encourages consideration of the therapeutic dyad as a two-person system – the 'bipersonal field' (Baranger and Baranger, 1966, 1990), in which the two protagonists act upon each other in equal degree, so that all events in the interaction are considered as products of the field, to which both participants contribute. In this way, the ambiguity of the therapeutic situation is highlighted, as 'a pair situation where all imaginable pair situations (as well as others) can be experienced, without acting any of them. Its mobility and indefiniteness are thus essential' (Baranger and Baranger, 1990, 344).

Systems theory conceptualizes the therapeutic dyad as 'a living system, whose properties belong to the whole, rather than to the constituent parts, and which arise from the interactions and relationships between the parts ... the properties of the parts are not intrinsic properties, but can be understood only within the context of the larger whole' (Capra, 1997: 29).

To reflect on the therapeutic interaction from a systemic perspective should not imply a depersonalization of the encounter. On the contrary, it places the therapist 'inside' the interaction, being fully and intensively with the Other, open to the possibilities for and challenges to herself through the encounter. Without this 'insideness', the ambiguity of the to-and-fro of the process is lost. Then the two-person system is no longer alive, and its demise closes off the possibility of dynamic change or development for either participant.

Taking the leading role in reflecting on the modes of 'being-together', the therapist attends to the unique, complex symphony of the interplay between the desires, fantasies, and anxieties of both herself and the client, and the therapeutic context or frame. Both client and therapist will tend to repeat the 'vicious cycles' of their own lives: it is the function of the therapist to rescue herself as well as the client, 'since both are participants in the same drama' (Baranger and Baranger, 1990, 345).

Such a drama will entail as much failure and retrogression as 'progress', as great a possibility for tragedy as for triumph, since 'being-together' remains a struggle for most practitioners. Having said that, we recognize the disastrous possibilities when a sense of 'being-together' is absent. Returning to an earlier passage, when the therapist attempts to 'cancel or change or alter or modify the other person in order to suit one's own good', or when the therapist 'attempts to fit the client into a formula, or conveys a sense of superiority', when the therapist attempts to deny the individuality of the person they are sitting with, the therapist has, in fact, turned away from her client (Laing, 1976).

Similarly the impact of the teacher on the learner, and the potential impact of all the learning, in any training, cannot be emphasized too strongly. The 'being-together' of teacher and learner demands a relinquishing of any claim to 'knowing' on the part of the teacher. The teacher who 'knows' indoctrinates rather than teaches, detracts from the stature of the Other and precludes the possibility of real meeting and real learning. What remains is the unmet demand of the Other. Those instances when a concept has been successfully struggled with and conveyed, when respect is met, when the exhilaration of learning permeates the room, so that fear, competition, and self-doubt shrivel in the corner – that is the being-together of teacher and learners. Those instances when a student stands her ground in disagreement, or confusion, demanding the teacher go that extra mile to unravel the learning – that is the being-together of teacher and learner. When the teacher is seen to make a mistake, in fact, or in judgement, when her fragility and fallibility are inescapably on public display and yet, rather than being diminished by this exposure, she is seen to remain open to learning, and that openness is received with graciousness by her students – that is the being-together of teacher and learners.

4
The Frame for Teaching/Learning

Contextualizing Psychotherapy

As a school kid, M used to inscribe her name in her exercise books thus:

> Mary MacCallum, 23 Alice St, Paisley, Scotland, Great Britain, Europe, the World, the Universe

She identified herself as a (minuscule) element existing in a hierarchy of contexts, starting from the self and radiating outwards to the edge of the known.

We recognize ourselves as 'implicated' in the world in different ways. The practice of psychotherapy, on the face of it shut away, hidden from the world, is a very intimate, profound way of implicating oneself firstly in the lives of the individuals who come to us, and further by the impact of that interaction with their worlds, and with the world at large. This chapter does not aim to encompass such an entirety, but will endeavour to describe some of the salient factors, both proximal and distal, that may affect and interact with what psychotherapy (and psychotherapy training) is understood to be, and how it is taught and learnt.

The psychotherapeutic interaction, despite its private, even 'clandestine' nature, does not take place in isolation from its context. As for psychotherapy, so much the more for psychotherapy training.

Social Context

How is psychotherapy, and its training modes, situated within the historical and political context of 'late capitalism'? Kovel (1988) levels the charge against psychotherapy that it is a distraction from social action – a placebo.

> Therapy has in some respects been even more successful than religion in deflecting energy from the need for radical social change ... even when pretending to be transcendent, the reward it dangles is no eschatological grappling with ultimates but an ultimately mundane, 'sensible' happiness, quite eligible for commodification. (Kovel, 1988: 121)

The historic failure of psychotherapy, he claims, has been that it has focused on the individual as an isolate, rather than addressing the interaction between the subjectivity thus unveiled and its context, the external socio-political experience within which therapy is situated, and by which it is largely formed.

He points to the colonization of subjectivity by twentieth-century capitalism to the extent that desire – the individual's day-dreaming – has become 'commodified': our values, our ambitions, our anxieties are subverted into a marketing oppor-tunity against which we have little resistance.

In the context of 'globalization' – a process of the continuous creation of new markets – there is a danger that the field of psychotherapy constitutes a further area of colonization, that it becomes itself a commodity – a product – one of a range of possible remedies against my sense of failure, a strategy to improve my own personal 'brand', rather than a way of exploring my disequilibrium in the world. Depending on the quality and properties of the therapeutic presence, the therapeutic dialogue may offer either a necessary critique of the social order or merely a new form of personal fetish, collusive in the manipulation of desire.

When we promote the chimera of 'self-development', when we propose a 'profession' of psychotherapy and engage in training psychotherapists, when we hold out the promise of therapy as a non-invasive 'cure' for a range of certified disorders, we make unjustified claims for the product. The only psychotherapy worth buying or selling is a limited psychotherapy that eschews a desire to 'cure' or to 'liberate', that entails a profound respect for the integrity and worth of the person, a critical psychotherapy that confines itself to 'the obstinate attempt to be-together with the Other', alongside a radical questioning, an examination of myself, my values, my life, my relationships, my world, and a challenge to the status quo.

> The heart of psychotherapy is what feels like a restoration of the self, a recognition of personal integrity, as I recover and reclaim my reflective capacity: 'a reflective subject is a critical, resistant subject'. (Kovel, 1988: 142)

The reflective, critical individual recognizes herself not merely as a member of the 'herd', pushed and pulled by the pressure to 'belong' and to participate in the communal life, but as a being who faces moment-to-moment responsibility for her choices and for the quality of her being, and for the discomfort in her being-in-the-world that such a responsibility engenders.

For we live in a fractured society, and feel paradoxically powerless despite inhabiting what is described as an 'advanced democracy' in which it is not easy to understand how responsibility can be actualized. As psychotherapists, we may, however, feel ourselves to belong to a 'community of persons', perhaps a profession, that can represent a common stance in relation to the continuing struggle to achieve meaning for ourselves in the world. Therefore it is inevitable that psychotherapy sits uncomfortably beside other 'professions' and disciplines, that it remains an 'odd job' likened to everything from 'secular priest' to 'prostitute', largely at odds with much of the social order. Consulting rooms are peopled by the fallout of the current social order.

Statutory Registration

The multitude of psychotherapeutic (and counselling) 'schools' mimic religious movements, or sects, with each different modality holding to its own language and set of rituals as a preferred version of 'the truth' which will 'save', or redeem adherents, practitioners or clients. Each modality generally has a founder, whose writings form a core 'scripture', back to which all other writings must refer; and each modality has reserved to itself the exclusive right to train would-be practitioners in the esoteric language/knowledge and (sometimes) techniques of its cultic practices.

Gregory Bateson (1958) points to a seemingly 'innate' tendency in units of societies or communities to 'split', or towards schism. He suggests that many ritualistic tendencies or social structures evolve as an effort to manage this 'innate' tendency to separate. Perhaps, then, this multifarious development is not necessarily to be deprecated, but to be managed and even celebrated.

And if a multiple vision is somehow an expression of a 'natural' tendency, it would be helpful – is indeed, essential – to see a greater willingness to tolerate difference, to see organizations increasingly develop the capacity to co-exist and to function side by side, without having to be at odds. We can even understand the whole complex field as somehow interconnected, capable of working in some fashion as a system of differentiated or interlocking cells. Is there not, in fact, a need for a multifarious vision of how to go about assisting people in addressing human dilemmas, since this chimes with the complexity of what it means to be human?

This multiple vision has contributed to the status of psychotherapy as a marginalized discipline, with training and registration of practitioners under the private ownership of an assorted collection of independent schools and training institutes, each securing and protecting their own territory and both subject to and distracted by the pressures of both the internal dynamics of the particular group and the external realities/politics of the field. For clients undertaking therapy, and for applicants for training, the task of choosing a modality of therapy or of training has involved comparison of different theoretical universes. While the diversity of visions reflects the 'chaotic' range of human meaning, it can be argued that working towards a degree of order and structure in the practice of psychotherapy would at least provide some signposts, some transparency, for potential learners and clients alike, bewildered by the choices they face and for a degree of consistency that would encourage teachers and practitioners to be accountable to their clients for their practice.

In the field of training, there is an increasing trend for courses provided by organizations across a range of perspectives to be linked with universities through validation arrangements. This affiliative relationship allows the training institution independence, and for diversity and creativity in relation to content and process, while the form of training is 'quality assured' by demonstrated adherence to the academic standards monitored by the university.

In Britain this trend has been paralleled by the slow and patient development over the past two decades of the United Kingdom Council for Psychotherapy (UKCP), the umbrella body for the broad range of psychotherapies in the UK. The UKCP, 'a national body seeking to organise a diversity of theoretical and practical orientations into a [professional] field of psychotherapy' (Figlio, 1993: 328), is committed to the achievement of a model of statutory professional registration of practitioners across a range of modalities that has been developed internally, as opposed to being imposed by government.

Statutory professional registration may, it is hoped, allow practitioners to present themselves to prospective clients/ customers as possessing a recognized qualification that attests their competence to practise psychotherapy. Statutory recognition implies some measure of agreement and transparency regarding what constitutes the required professional and academic standards for qualification and registration.

Yet we are, at the same time, keenly aware of the dangers of statutory registration: not only is it likely to serve more to protect therapists and therapy organizations than clients, but it may support and encourage a 'medical' and 'scientific' model of psychotherapy[1] (a misleading and outdated paradigm of medicine as an expert, evidence-based 'science'). It may therefore also constrain the activities of those who practise on a voluntary and/or part-time basis and may detract from the creativity and 'artistry' of practitioners.

> Practitioner therapeutic effectiveness is surely a highly complex, empirically immeasurable and ultimately mysterious process, with a multitude of variables, many or most of them of the 'intangible variety'; it is the

---

1. As a profession 'allied to medicine'.

practitioner's freshness of energy, enthusiasm and associated interest-in-the-other that may be a far more important, even decisive 'ingredient' in therapist effectiveness than has heretofore been recognized (House, 2001: 14).

Paul Gordon also expresses our reservations about 'the lure of professionalism'. Noticing that we generally use the adjective 'professional' as a compliment, he goes on to draw on Illich's (1977) critique of 'disabling professions', founded on a general delusional and infantilizing belief in an orderly universe in which 'people had problems, experts had solutions, and scientists measured imponderables such as abilities and needs'. Professions go further than trade associations, he claims.

> Indeed the true mark of the professional is precisely the authority to define someone as a client, to determine that person's need and to prescribe the appropriate treatment. The professionals assert secret knowledge about human nature, knowledge which only they have the power to dispense. The bodies of the 20th century professional specialist, Illich claimed, are more deeply entrenched than a Byzantine bureaucracy, endowed with wider competencies than any shaman, and equipped with a tighter hold over those who they claim as victims than any Mafia ... (Gordon, 1999: 34)

Gordon claims, with justice, that professions come into existence in order to protect their members, and that clients or patients have had little satisfaction from attempts to complain or seek redress. Concepts such as 'authority' and 'expertise' support the illusion that the 'problems' of one individual can be 'solved' by another, and sit uncomfortably alongside the definition of psychotherapy as 'a particular type of conversation with those we see in a mutual attempt to understand their difficulties in living their lives'. As he points out, 'A conversation that makes sense to some can seem absurd to others. It would be a strange and horrible world if certain kinds of conversation were to be controlled or even prohibited' (*ibid*: 33–5).

Steve Gans points to the 'secular religion' of therapy, and questions its status as a profession – 'It's not at all clear that one ought to be paid for this work' (Gans and Redler, 2001: 83).

M: For me, there is greater honour in undertaking the work as a professional rather than as some kind of 'secular priest', since the power of the professional is mitigated by the payment of a fee. In a properly regulated profession, there is the possibility that unsatisfactory service will not deserve a fee. There is recognition that an exchange takes place, that you and I meet; that if I am 'for-you' in a therapeutic fashion, I will be worthy of the fee that you pay me. We remain equals. I would argue that there is a danger that I may believe that the ongoing free dispensation of my 'being-for-the-Other' elevates me above the necessity for food and shelter, for the need for an income, and thus constitutes me as a 'higher being', which may render me beyond criticism. If both professional and client are interdependent in terms of the rendering of a service for a fee, the power relations remain within a healthy spectrum.

H: But is the choice 'professional' or 'secular priest'? There are other metaphors and symbols. I respect your views. This work is riddled with dangers no matter how or where it is situated. But I also see that for many the lure of professionalism – the acceptance into the world of 'experts' – panders to the childish need for acknowledgement and a place alongside the 'grown-ups'. Far preferable for all concerned that we struggle to maintain our independence, that we remain unencumbered.

M: Yet we work with vulnerable individuals, who need protection or, at least, a means of protest or redress against the inevitable failures. I see the intention of the overall project of professionalization, for all its pitfalls and dangers, as allowing psychotherapists a system of self-regulation, rather than being further marginalized and patronized by other, more 'scientifically' orientated interest groups.

Moreover, the regulatory climate of the professions in Britain seems to have entered a period of change: as with professions such as medicine, law and social work, within the last few years, the professional psychotherapy bodies (BACP,[2] UKCP,[3] BPS[4]) have more explicitly engaged with their regulatory responsibilities and have begun to promote, if not justice, then at least a limited arena for clients and students to express dissent, through the requirement for agencies and organizations to have, promulgate and implement standardized complaints and grievance procedures. Professional and training organizations, through these procedures, are required to be open to a degree of lay scrutiny of their criteria and practices that offers some protection against abuse and exploitation that sadly – given the human tendency to 'cheat' (see Chapter 6) – too often flourish in the arena of private, 'clandestine' relationships. Codes and procedures, bureaucratic, cumbersome and fallible as they are, are the necessary corollary to our commitment to an ethical endeavour, and to our vigilance concerning the power relation within the encounter.

M: It is in my view, the drive to 'professionalism', at least in part, with its possibility of a regulatory structure of quality standards, codes, procedures and organizational infrastructure,

2. British Association for Counselling and Psychotherapy.
3. United Kingdom Council for Psychotherapy.
4. British Psychological Society.

which has created a 'frame' for a commonality *in practice* of psychotherapy, thus supporting a willingness of different modalities to engage in dialogue together. Of course there is, as always, a self-serving motivation in all of this, but the honourable dimension of the professionalization of psychotherapy is that it reflects the internalization of an ideal that is ethical and trustworthy. The ideal is articulated in a code of ethics, while a code of practice provides for a 'transparent' monitoring of compliance with the aspiration (Figlio, 2002) through both professional and lay involvement. Through these codes, clients, and, indeed, students and colleagues, who feel themselves to have been, at best, short-changed, and at worst, abused or exploited, may seek, if not redress, then at least acknowledgement, of a possible wrong done to them. Without them, those without power do not have the means to make themselves heard.

H: But in fact the safeguard of a bureaucracy and infrastructure created in order to protect against the many dangers of our work is, more often than not, 'illusion' (see Chapter 6). I appreciate the intentions of 'the drive to professionalism'. I fully endorse the notion of 'self-regulation', however impossible it may actually be at any other than an individual level, but in this regard, psychotherapy is following a model that has failed badly elsewhere. One only has to look to the legal system from which the structures you describe emanate. Conciliation, mediation, these are methods that attempt to incorporate an element of the dialogic; the danger is that we fall into the old adversarial trap. I think that is antithetical to what we are about.

And on the darker side, we referred earlier to the 'colonization of subjectivity' and could add that, for some, registration and regulation are an attempt at the 'colonization of psychotherapy' – no longer the revolutionaries sitting behind closed doors, but 'professionals' sitting beside other 'professionals'. In truth there is clearly a strand within the psychotherapeutic community, beginning with Freud himself, who desire this position, and are prepared to pay the price. I believe it is important to resist such temptation.

M: No safeguard, no 'solution', but a means of articulating 'iatrogenic' damage in the presence of responsible others who have the power either to impose sanctions or at least to ensure that the voice of the 'victim' is heard. I have had experience, through membership of ethics committees, of working with dissatisfied clients and trainees who feel themselves to have been harmed and hurt by their involvement with therapy/ therapy training. We clearly need some form of framework in place to be able to address these grievances. We recognize that what has happened that has caused pain can never be undone, but that, nevertheless, justice demands our willingness to listen to these concerns as part of the overall dialogue. Without the means to complain, the damage (unfair treatment, exploitation, abuse) is hidden, remains secret, allowing practitioners to remain oblivious to harm done, and to leave the responsibility for 'failure' wholly with the client.

As with other professions, we may be in danger of fostering the illusion that 'doctors can (or shortly will be able to) cure everything'. People are being punished for failures, or mistakes made in the course of treatment – medical technology fosters this illusion – when, of course, humans are fallible; there will always be mistakes, there will always be failures. We cannot legislate against human (or technological) failure.

But progress made in developing a common language is beginning to render at least some aspects of the 'mysterious' therapeutic interaction more transparent. The determination, in line with European trends, to develop psychotherapy training as an academically and professionally rigorous discipline, entered at a postgraduate level, aims to present psychotherapy as a field for critical inquiry, and may reduce the factionalism induced by doctrinal loyalties, sketching out possible common ground between psychotherapy and other disciplines. This is a vital and necessary development, which sits alongside and questions an approach which espouses a view of psychotherapy as radical and ethical, yet, at its essence, 'only' a 'particular form of conversation' between two, unique, persons.

The Training Organization

> We speak of families as though we all knew what families
> are ... The more one studies family dynamics, the more
> unclear one becomes as to the ways family dynamics
> compare and contrast with the dynamics of other groups
> not called families ... As with dynamics, so with
> structure (patterns, more stable and enduring than
> others); again, comparisons and generalisations must be
> very tentative. (Laing, 1976a: 3)

Just as 'there is no such thing as a baby ...' (Winnicott, 1964), perhaps it may be useful to propose that there's no such thing as a learner, there is only a teacher/learner unit, a two-person unit, or at least a unit made up of the learner and the teaching institution; a system that is interconnected by means of the initial agreement between the two partners. And, since the teacher also carries the institution in her and with her into the interaction with the learner, no discussion of training can be complete without consideration of the *immediate* context in which training is situated and how the modalities of training shape the learning of the learner.

If the efficacy of therapy depends largely on the nature and quality of the therapeutic relationship, it may be that the efficacy of a therapy training will depend as much on the nature and quality of the relationship between the training organization and the trainee, as on the larger 'frame' of the political and social context in which the institution has its being. The environment within which teaching and learning psychotherapy takes place shapes the learning, and among the determinants of that environment are the motivations, intentions and indeed the emotional and behavioural patterns of those who are members of the institution and participate in its activities. The institution is more than the sum of its members, but it constitutes and is constituted by the 'ghost world' of those who, however unknowingly, influence its operation.

As beings-in-relation, all individuals in some aspect of their lives tend to coalesce into neo-familial groups either as a way of playing out or 'working through' the patterns of connectedness we learnt through our experience of the family nexus, or simply because it is the 'natural' way of being in relation. A psychotherapy (training) institution is, clearly, such a group; primarily the group of people who form the staff who support and deliver the therapy training, together with their relation to the organization's history and its 'custom and practice'. 'Each institution is a portion of the individual's personality ... identity is always, wholly or partially, institutional, in the sense that at least one part of the identity always shapes itself by belonging to a group' (Bleger, 1967, 1990: 420). The 'personality' of the organization is also informed by its physical, geographical, social and political setting.

Kernberg proposed that there are four models of psychoanalytic training institutes:

1. an art academy training expert craftspeople and bringing artistic talents to fruition;
2. a technical trade school focused on learning a 'clearly defined skill or trade, with no emphasis on artistic creativity';

3. a monastery or seminary model that treats psychoanalysis as a religious system;
4. a university college model that aims at the transmission, exploration and generation of knowledge and methodological tools for the creation of new knowledge. (Kernberg, 1986: 809, 810; cited in Kirsner, 2000: 4)

The psychoanalytic sector, in agreement with Gans and Redler (2001), has adhered, throughout its history, to the apprenticeship model, with the training analysis as the crucial arena for learning: a training therapist and a clinical supervisor monitor the internal world of the trainee. Kirsner claims that the training institution as seminary, wherein psychoanalysis is treated as a 'religious' discipline, has contributed to the decline of the status of psychoanalysis, highlighting the problem that 'a basically humanistic discipline has conceived and touted itself as a positivist science while organising itself institutionally as a religion' (Kirsner, 2000: 233).

> Through the medium of the training analysis, the transmission of important aspects of psychoanalysis often takes the form of an esoteric pipeline of sorts through which analytic truth is transmitted, from Freud on down, from analyst to analyst. This involves the process of anointment of those analysts – training analysts – deemed good enough to be the 'real', *echt* psychoanalysts. Training analysts, in turn, anoint their candidates through the medium of the training analysis. (*Ibid*: 4–5)

This approach to training 'is blind to the unconscious determinants of the conscious activities of these mini-societies within which psychotherapists learn and practise' (Figlio, 1993: 325). Kirsner describes the American psychoanalytic institutions he studied as closed shops. Their solid walls have kept them sealed off and mysterious to the outside world … Authoritarian cliques, power struggles and intrigues have predominated within the institutes. Institute life has been secret, the subject of rumour rather than knowledge. (Kirsner, 2000: 2)

Such a closed shop leaves trainees exposed to the vagaries of their teacher's 'particular form of madness', and no doubt elements of this pattern are replicated in many psychotherapy institutions. Somewhere implicit in the notion that one has a special insight into what training should be, or that one possesses esoteric knowledge not vouchsafed to lesser practitioners, is an unhealthy, omnipotent and 'salvationist' tendency (no doubt the present authors are not exempt) that must be mitigated against through openness to independent, external scrutiny and submission to training standards held in common with different modalities.

However, where training is orientated towards university standards and criteria, there may be a real risk that experiential and practical aspects of training might be downplayed in response to the bias towards academic success.

The expression 'therapy industry' (Gans and Redler, 2001) says something about scale. In order for the institutions to survive and thrive, they arguably must grow to a scale that may detract from their primary purpose, that of the provision of a setting in which individuals may develop their capacity to be-with another.

There is tension, too, between measurement of 'knowledge' and understanding and the attempt of both teacher and learner to 'be-together'. Where the universities have become involved in training, adherence to a theoretical position may be considered less important than the demonstration of mastery of a set of professional competencies. The pursuit of a guarantee of quality for psychotherapy training through academic excellence may detract from the 'unlearning' that is required in order to achieve satisfactory mastery of 'vigilant passivity', 'negative capability', or the ability to be-with, but, on the contrary, is likely to encourage a willing tendency to view the therapist as an 'expert', as 'the one who knows' over against an increasingly infantilized client.

M: As we talked about the place of theory, you referred to the cultural distinction that is made, the privileging of matters of the mind, the separating off of the intellect. We seek to legitimize what we do through conceptualizing and theorizing; this has to be part of the training because we say so. We thus elevate ourselves, and the profession, bringing about a hierarchical-ization of the profession, the industry, and thus maintaining our place in it.

H: I remember the artist David Hockney speaking of his time at the Slade (Art School) and how his work was not appreciated until he found the abstract words to describe it.

Most therapy training organizations have functioned as some combination of trade school and seminary, but with aspirations to the art academy and/or university model; the development of university-based training brings both benefits and disadvantages, but clearly emphasizes and supports this aspiration.

The adoption of a combination of the art academy and the university college model may encourage the organization to be an 'open system', with transparent regulations, open to external scrutiny and gaining the input of both 'expert' and 'lay' advice and evaluation. It also offers a brake on the power wielded by teacher over learner, with systems that ensure accountability, codes of ethics that seek to articulate transparent values, and codes of practice that offer a 'safety-net' of checks and balances which contain and constrain the power of individuals.

Stanton points to the positive aspects of the connection with the university and its traditions: 'the obligation to research all points of view, to encourage debate between differing and opposing points of view, and finally, to encourage interdisciplinarity and the creative interplay of arts and sciences in any particular field', which will encourage a move away from 'doctrinaire and seemingly self-evident views of clinical work towards the enigmatic and polysemic richness and diversity of psychotherapy work in all its contexts' (Stanton, 1993: 234).

Figlio clearly articulates the tensions:

> How does a training organisation both support the emerging identity of the trainee psychotherapist and maintain a critical eye on indicators of achievement? What kind of moral language speaks of the necessity, as an indicator of excellence, to judge trainees to have failed or to strip members of their membership? Who is responsible for the form that the exclusive and overseeing organisation – a group of peers who are also the object of aspiration – will take in the trainee's mind? Does the relationship between organisation and trainee, with many of its reality aspects distilled out through continuous mutual projection and introjection, invade the teaching, supervision and monitoring processes? Does it create a monstrous collective psyche, and how is it passed down through the generations and embedded in theoretical schisms? (Figlio, 1993: 325)

Training institutions must implement a process of selection of candidates for training which is rigorous in its demand for applicants to have an initial capacity for self-reflection, and to demonstrate a critical attitude to theories regarding what it means to be human, together with a consistently self-critical readiness to explore their motivation to train. Given these attributes, it is vital that those responsible for the selection of candidates for training are open to a sense of the possibilities inherent in a wide diversity of individuals, not simply those who have had, for example, prior experience either in psychology or in the 'helping professions'. The greater the range of human diversity in the training group, the greater the richness and depth of the training, which in turn will engender and encourage creative dialogue at all levels.

Equally, the institution, once the decision to accept a candidate is made, assumes a heavy responsibility, to watch over the unfolding process, in order to allow the psychotherapist to emerge, to act as the cradle for the developing chrysalis, to provide a facilitative environment, a 'secure base', a 'maternal holding'. Yet there are individuals for whom this process fails to unfold in the hoped-for manner; and it is then the responsibility of the institution to have measures in place which, while going to the utmost to support openness to possibilities for improvement, are also clear and timely in indicating when necessary learning is not achieved. Not all those who undertake training should necessarily expect to succeed; 'failure' must be allowed, and must be managed in a clear and accountable fashion, so that the conditions for failure are transparent, and trainees are made aware as early and as clearly as possible of the manner of their falling short of the criteria for 'success'.

The two-person teacher/learner, or teaching institution/learner system is interconnected by means of the initial agreement between the two partners. The teacher also carries the institution in her and with her into the interaction. And this reality can create difficult moments that are often the moments of judgement, of evaluation, where the tension, the anxiety surrounding the experience of being judged or of asserting a negative judgement, interferes with an open, person-to-person meeting simply because of the asymmetrical power relation.

When a person-to-person meeting becomes impossible, one may reach a 'last-resort' situation, where all that is left is to fall back on the authority, the 'parental' edict: 'not in my house'.

It's important to grapple with the negatives in the situation. We're all aware, in the teaching profession, of the greater degree of willingness of disappointed learners to resort to litigation, against either teachers or the institutions. With that awareness comes a tendency in us to self-protectiveness, a 'playing safe'. It becomes more difficult to deal with dissent or subversion. We may understand an individual's disruptiveness as a form of resistance or sabotage – part of the ongoing relationship or inter-action – but it may become more difficult to hold firm to our understanding rather than take flight into a defensive position. The whole educational sector, along with others, is currently concerned with procedures, guidelines and criteria that encourage transparency and give clarity regarding the 'rules' governing what we do. Yet this may also encourage us to take refuge in the 'book' when confronted with difficulties, rather than stand forth and address the difficulties with courage and confidence in a dialogic approach.

The encounter then, ironically, becomes the opposite of what we are proposing as a collaboration, a coalition; and yet it becomes necessary to come to terms, because if we don't both parties will be damaged … There may be times, then, when something has clearly gone wrong with the process: something has not been heard or something has not been said. It must be recognized that this may be a matter of cowardice, a failure of dialogue on the part of the teacher, the powerful one, who then retreats to this last-resort position of asserting authority.

In this situation, the institution or the teacher has to take responsibility for saying to the student, 'Unless you do so and so, you will not be able to qualify, etc.' That's a really hard thing to say, and it's harder because it's a very difficult thing to put into concrete terms, and that's why to some extent we dodge it. The difficulty remains: how do we show, with justice, clarity and fairness, what it is that somebody is failing to do, and what they must do to move from a fail judgement to a pass judgement?

H: Part of the task is to create an atmosphere where learners can openly work with their vulnerable aspects, and not always have the fear of assessment hanging over them. Individual teachers, within the institution, have the onus of creating that learning atmosphere, which ideally would not include concepts of pass and fail. How do we measure someone's ability to be with another in such absolute, concrete terms? Is it not better as teachers and learners to create a situation in which it is possible to participate in the process of considering the consequences and repercussions of different ways of being – in other words, facilitating independent ethical thinking and learning? Such learning can hopefully be integrated and taken with the prospective therapist into their working lives.

Working phenomenologically, I'm able to say: 'This is what I see ... I'm not telling you that this is good, bad or indifferent – let's think about it together.' There is a parallel with the degree to which the teacher can put herself on the line, recognizing: 'I know this will be uncomfortable; you're not going to like me. God knows what the repercussions are going to be, but this is what is going on, so I'd better say it.'

M: So you have to have confidence enough to believe in your

own judgement, or your own perception, in your phenomenological terminology.

H: My point, I suppose, is that in those instances, although I
can never entirely suspend my views, what I'm attempting to do
is not present judgements, but rather have the courage to present
observations, to say what I see ...

For the training organization retains ongoing responsibility to
potential clients for the practice of those whom it trains: clients
who experience professional or ethical shortcomings or failures in
therapists must be able to trust that their interests will be at the
forefront of concern. The organization must exact, as the price of
this continuing responsibility, its members' commitment to
competence and ethical practice, and it must be ready to be
rigorous in holding its alumni to account for such a
commitment.

Members of a training organization, both teachers and admin-
istrators, also carry the responsibility for the form that the
organization, the 'exclusive and overseeing' internalized parental
representation in the mind of the 'infant' trainee, will take. The
dynamics of the organization, as played out through the
processes of teaching, supervision and evaluation, will be replicated, to some or other extent, as a 'ghost-world' (Bleger,
1967,1990: 420) or infrastructure of professional attitudes and
motivations, which will permeate the future practice and
professional life of the trainee.

A Learning Community

'The Outfit' (the Cambridge Society of Psychotherapy), in
Cambridge, has sought to develop a community of learning
in which the student is given the opportunity – and the

responsibility – for using a facilitating environment to learn to practise therapy (Lomas, 2001: 123–4).

H: I'm reminded of a conversation I had some time ago, to do with Jewish history: about the experience of 'homelessness' and what, paradoxically, it may actually facilitate. Having already moved my consulting room three times during my career, I carry this intangible, possibly grandiose, hope that I can 'hold' my client, that it doesn't really matter where we are, that if we're together, the rapport that we have created together will sustain us, and that the relationship can survive the dis-location of the move, the experience of becoming homeless, and then re-creating a 'home' for the work.

M: I can see how it resonates with your work around marginal-ization (Goldenberg 1997), and with the thread of meaning relating to how so many colleagues are, or feel themselves to be, homeless or dis-located in a geographical sense. And I'm reminded of how Albany (Shakespeare, *King Lear*) described his wife Goneril as 'dis-branched':

> She that herself will sliver and disbranch
> From her material sap, perforce must wither
> And come to deadly use. (Act 4, scene 2, lines 34–6)

I wonder about the influence on us of the nature of our attachment to, our identification with, 'the group'. Do we have a need to 're-branch' ourselves, if you like, to find, or make, a group with which we are comfortable to claim relationship? Can this group, this community, this organization, be 'good-enough' as a holding environment for me, so that I can be that for others?

H: There is of course a strong thread of meaning in the history of psychoanalysis around exile and homelessness, which contributes to the intangible qualities inherent in the endeavour. The other side of the 'exile' experience is the sense that so many therapists have of 'coming home', of finding a place, a community of like-minded people, and the excitement and relief of feeling 'at home'.

The School of Psychotherapy and Counselling at Regent's College seeks to provide:

> a learning environment which allows competing and
> diverse models to be considered both conceptually and
> experientially so that their areas of interface and
> divergence can be exposed, considered and clarified. This
> aim espouses the value of holding the tension between
> contrasting and often contradictory ideas, of 'playing with'
> their experiential possibilities and of allowing a paradoxical
> security which can 'live with' and at times even thrive in
> the absence of final and fixed truths. (SPC, 2002: 6/7)

The primary responsibility and task of the psychotherapy training institution is to provide a 'safe-enough' environment for both teachers and learners, providing a 'cradling' that will enable trainees to experience and to practise 'being-together' with each other, and which will facilitate the unfolding of their reparative and learning capacities. The quality of the practical, or experiential, aspects of training is therefore crucial. The environment of training, including the human environment, must promote an atmosphere and ethos of trust within the training group, whereby trainees both support and challenge each other in a way that encourages deeply personal learning.

It is all too easy to forget that the institution *is* the people; one hears members talking about the organization as if it were a person, dissociating themselves from 'the way things are'. Bleger points out that '[w]hat is always there is never noticed until it is missing ... There is no awareness of what is always present' (1967, 1990: 420). Thus, for teachers, it takes a real leap of imaginative realization to encompass their identity as an element of the institutional structure: the way individuals are, with colleagues and with learners, communicates aspects of the organization's underlying purpose and values.

It is also fatally easy to deny that being situated as an individual with responsibility for and power over other individuals within the institution constructs me as a part of the structure, as a subject of that institution, rather than a passive object of its practices. The larger the organization, and the less power I perceive myself to have within the organization, the less I can be aware of my role as a 'pillar' of the institution. Yet we all, teachers and learners alike, form the outward manifestation of the institution. There is bound to be dissonance between actual modes of being together and the organization's manifest stated ethos and values, and this dissonance should be the subject of ongoing reflection and participative discussion.

We are all so much more aware of how an organization's profile can be consciously 'spun', through attention to the 'brand', through the development of the 'mission statement' and all the paraphernalia of 21st century image-building. What we are less careful of is how the implicit aspects of an organization's 'personality' can be evidenced through its procedures, its style of communication, through the 'body-language' of its everyday administration and 'housekeeping', as well as through the nature of its physical setting and the physical environment it provides.

Isobel Menzies Lyth proposed that 'the success and viability of a social institution are intimately connected with the techniques it uses to contain anxiety' (Menzies Lyth, 1988; 78). The primary task of the institution is, she claimed, subverted by the social defence system developed to combat the anxiety created by that task: 'the social defence system represented the institutional-isation of very primitive defence mechanisms, a main characteristic of which is that they facilitate the evasion of anxiety but contribute little to its true modification and reduction' (*ibid*: 77).

Like nurses, psychotherapists deliberately and consciously put themselves in the way of the pain and suffering of others, and take on the task of professionally addressing that pain and suffering. Any psychotherapy institution will represent at once both the best attempt of a group of people to promote and provide high standards of service, and the worst of their efforts to defend against the anxieties thus aroused. The primary task of the psychotherapy training organization and of its constituent members is to 'cradle the chrysalis' that is the fledgling psychotherapist; the organization must find ways of being alert to how its secondary task – the 'evasion of anxiety' – may become a greater priority than the benefit of trainees.

The context within which individuals learn to become psychotherapists must provide a 'safe-enough' potential space, that can facilitate a 'playing with' the experiential possibilities of contrasting and often contradictory ideas in order to be able to 'live with' and at times even thrive in the absence of final and fixed truths (SFC, 2000, 6–7).

The analogy of the chrysalis denotes the awareness that the key factor in the development of a psychotherapist is the unfolding of the individual's own creativity:

> It is in playing and only in playing that the child or adult is able to be creative and use the whole personality, and it is only in being creative that the individual discovers the self. (Winnicott, 1999: 54)

109

It is up to the training institution to facilitate such a process, to safeguard such an innocent yet courageous endeavour, providing the 'cradling' that the trusting trainee needs and deserves.

5
The Substance of Teaching/Learning

If I have told you these details about the asteroid, and made a note of its number for you, it is on no account of the grown-ups and their ways. Grown ups love figures. When you tell them that you've made a new friend, they never ask you any questions about essential matters. They never say to you, 'What does his voice sound like? What games does he love best? Does he collect butterflies?' Instead, they demand: 'How old is he? How many brothers has he? How much does he weigh? How much does his father make?' Only from these figures do they think they have learned anything about him.

If you were to say to the grown-ups: 'I saw a beautiful house made of rosy brick, with geraniums in the windows and doves on the roof,' they would not be able to get any idea of that house at all. You would have to say to them: 'I saw a house that cost £4000.' Then they would exclaim: 'Oh, what a pretty house that is!'

Just so, you might say to them: 'The proof that the little prince existed is that he was charming, that he laughed, and that he was looking for a sheep. If anybody wants a sheep, that is proof that he exists.' And what good would it do to tell them that? They would shrug their shoulders, and treat you like a child. But if you said to them: 'The planet he came from is Asteroid B-612', then they would be convinced and leave you in peace from their questions.

They are like that. One must not hold it against them. Children should always show great forbearance toward grown-up people. (Saint-Exupéry, 1945: 17–18)

What are the 'essential matters' that should comprise a psychotherapy training?

A Foot on the Road

Some of those who apply to enter training seem to feel that they know what's involved in becoming a therapist; that there is a givenness about the programme, or about the theoretical components of training – a 'knowledge' to be transmitted. The only advantage of knowledge in this context, however, is that it may enable us to recognize just how little we know; the first task of training is to blow away the cobwebs, these attitudes and assumptions, to say 'open your mind'. In selecting people to enter training we look for a willingness to undergo a process that is as much about un-learning, un-knowing, un-certainty, as much as it is about developing the skills and capacities that will allow one to practise as a 'good-enough' therapist. There's clearly an important element of self-selection, and that must be respected, but also tested. Would-be therapists must be willing to 'leave home' and set out on a journey, of which the destination is uncertain, the terrain is uncharted, the reliability of the mode of transport is untested, and one's companions are as likely as not to be the usual suspects, like Christian's companions in *Pilgrim's Progress*, rogues, vagabonds, charlatans and liars, all just trying to be good.

When I make a decision about whether to offer an applicant a training place, even at the initial (foundation) level, my attitude has to be that it's my decision, at this moment in time, as to whether this individual may be capable of becoming a therapist. It is all too easy to duck that responsibility, trusting that someone else will, later in the process, find an opportunity to say 'no'. It's entirely appropriate to utilize the widest possible interpretation of entry criteria, in order to honour the possibilities in each individual for radical learning and development, and for a rich and diverse range of life experience to contribute to the co-creation of the learning community. Yet it is also necessary to be vigilant regarding the limits of a safe environment. Participants in training may only be able to bear so much reality … So we must always be careful to make clear to applicants that we cannot offer guarantees about the outcome of training.

In the Introduction we described the competent professional psychotherapist: 'one who is consistently able to provide and facilitate a relationship in and through which a client may be encouraged to undertake a process of self-exploration and self-discovery. The therapist's primary aim is to achieve a 'being-with' the Other: to sustain a quality of attending to her client which will allow the client to disclose himself to himself, while the therapist remains herself relatively unknown. The development of such a relationship requires her to be at once professionally 'neutral' and yet to demonstrate in her behaviour a kind of 'love' for her client (Chapter 5).

In this context, hackles and antennae may rise at the use of the word 'love'. Love is not a simple concept. But we believe that there is an underlying love for and faith in humanity at the core of our work. Such an attitude we propose should be given recognition as a valid driving force for interest in this field.

Self-interest must be examined: any form of professional involvement in the 'caring' industries is subject to the desire for power, and each and every action must be considered for its ethical implications, as must each individual's motivation for such a 'career' choice. The corollary is that any training is long, expensive, and arduous, the outcome uncertain; there is every justification for high levels of anxiety and an enhanced vulnerability to damage and exploitation. As we have proposed earlier, the only ethical and humane response to such a situation of unequal power on the part of the teacher, and ultimately the training organization, must be an attitude of 'care'.

Fundamental to the enterprise of psychotherapy training promoted by this book is the insistence that, as a practitioner, I must carefully and consistently subject myself to rigorous professional 'supervision' that examines the self-serving aspects of my contribution to the interaction with clients. This collaborative approach seeks to minimize the 'subjection' of clients and students to my covert agendas and unexplored desires. Applicants for training must indicate that, to some degree, they are cognizant of the nature of the task they undertake: they must already have an initial capacity for self-reflection, and demonstrate an interest in and a curiosity about what it means to be human.

Learning to Walk

'In the beginning is the word ...' (John 1: 1)

The aim and purpose of the initial stage of training is both to introduce participants to the mode of being that underpins psychotherapy and to allow an exploration of this realm and of associated ideas to a point where it may become clear to the participant whether or not she should undertake further training. An additional possible, not-to-be-despised, outcome to this level of training is that, by its completion, participants will have learnt enough to make an informed choice of therapist!

H: What comes to mind as I think about the substance of teaching, is the sort of hierarchical thinking that often applies within education generally, not just within the field of therapy education. I have always thought that it is a big mistake to give higher status to 'higher levels of teaching' where I think you really need the best quality possible at the beginning. I don't think there is enough attention given to the quality of input that is being offered at the very preliminary stage.

M: We call it the foundation ...

H: And it's meant to be a foundation! I would like to see more emphasis and more status given to this initial stage.

M: Yet this is a problem with the attempt to give the profession this sense of credibility attached to the academic qualification – the postgraduate level of training; that the higher the degree, the higher is the status of the teacher ... The higher education way of doing things inevitably leans towards a privileging of the mind and the intellectual capacity rather than the whole person.

H: And this is so much more than an intellectual endeavour ... The psychotherapeutic manner of being includes the development of alertness to existence, awareness of self and Other that allows a sense of interpersonal process, the rhythm of active speech action and an even more active 'passivity' of listening. Students will become aware that clients need to proceed at their own pace, but that therapists proceed at the client's pace. Thus the training organization has an obligation also to pay attention to the rhythm of the student:

> ... the training practice provides for alternating periods
> of immersion/receptivity, and of conceptual elaboration

of material. The fostering of artistic 'reverie' alternates with scientific reflection and evaluation of the material; and this dual mode of learning is then transmitted into an analogous mode of teaching. (Campart, 1996: 54, cited in Williams, 1999, 127–35)

Listening

The first step in an initial course is to learn, through doing, the radical art of listening. What do we mean by listening? One offers oneself and one's presence as the context in which the other speaks, but holds oneself still – quite literally – to refrain from action through speech, to 'allow' the discourse of the Other to flow, to hesitate, to become stuck, to free itself, to gather into a deep pool of silence. Even when the experience of speaking to an Other without the limitation of the Other's 'for-me' response terrifies the speaker into a stuttering and beseeching silence, there can often be a paradoxical reassurance in the listener's silent witnessing and allowing of the discomfort.

Paul Gordon lists those who have contributed to our enhanced understanding of what listening involves:

> For Heidegger, listening is paying 'thoughtful attention to simple things', for Bakhtin it is 'responsive understanding'; for Gadamer, 'Anyone who listens is fundamentally open. Belonging together always also means being able to listen to one another'. So listening is a stance, a position, an attitude that we can choose to take – or not … (Gordon, 1999: 73)

Attending

> Attending is a phenomenon that appears to have a
> number of effects which are like environmental
> affordances. It can provide a holding, it can provide a
> kind of spaciousness, it can provide a kind of close
> contact, it can provide a sense of confirmation. In all
> these ways, attention can offer a place or a sense of being
> and relatedness. (Pearmain, 2001: 127)

I gather my self together, and offer that gathered being as a resource to the Other; I enter the state of reverie, a form of attentiveness that does not exclude a drift or flow of rumination, fantasy, bodily sensation, fleeting half-awareness of perceptions, thoughts, associations. It is not only a personal and private event, but an intersubjective one, since the form it takes, and its content, is also shaped by the Other. My guiding intention in this is to be-for.

Hearing

> ... if we are attending to what we hear, without other
> distraction, and if we are truly open to what we hear,
> then we are listening. We are not trying to *understand*
> what we hear but, rather, are allowing ourselves to be
> touched by it – or indeed not touched by it – and
> surprised by it. A true listener hears not just the melody,
> what is most obvious, and is not distracted by this, but
> the many layers of sound that constitute the piece as a
> whole. A true listener hears, therefore, the conversations
> that go on within any piece. A listener who is trying to be

true to what she is hearing does not compare what she is listening to with something else. At least she does not approach a piece in terms of what she is already familiar with, although such comparisons may suggest themselves in the process of listening. She is trying to hear the piece in its own terms, on its own ground. (Gordon, 1999: 73–4)

The analogy of music well illuminates the activity of the therapist: I will not hear unless my ears have become trained and tuned, until my mind has, through practice, become permeable to the multi-levelled, manifold aspects of possible meaning and shade in one little word, phrase or throw-away muttered aside. Hearing involves being able to use an inchoate semi-under-standing to unearth a 'Rosetta Stone' – a key, which will facilitate connections and links in the speaker's 'material'. Hearing requires us to set aside our own defences to the point where we can bear to hear ourselves, often indirectly, guided or criticized by our clients. It may also be useful for me actually to 'hear' what I as therapist say ...

However hard we listen, we will often fail to hear; our own blocks, defences, deficiencies will prevent us from picking up nuances, hidden meanings, non-verbal or indirect communi-cation, whether on the part of a client or in our own contribution.

Waiting

I must allow time for a process of attunement to the Other and to the 'now' of the interaction for both myself and my client; I must manage and tolerate my own anxiety in such a way that it can be put on one side, avoiding the compulsion to understand, to make sense. Waiting opens up the potential space between therapist and client which will allow for a 'rhythm of withdrawal and return which constitutes the universal and necessary pattern of personal development' (MacMurray, 1957, 1991: 88) or for the distance without which there can be no relation: '. . . one can enter into relation only with a being which has been set at a distance, more precisely, has become an independent opposite' (Buber, 1998: 50).

Movement, change, the client's own creativity, will make use of or fill the space provided:

> If only we can wait the patient arrives at understanding creatively and with immense joy, and now I enjoy this joy more than I used to enjoy the sense of having been clever. I think I interpret mainly to let the patient know the limits of my understanding. (Winnicott, 1971, 1999: 86, 87)

Self-restraint

An early lesson is to learn how not to speak in order better to listen; the second to learn when not to speak; the third is to gain mastery over myself in order to refrain from speaking, sometimes when I am most strongly impelled to do so. Even if the statement or comment is only delayed until a later point in that or another session, when a 'cue' is offered again, or until, best of all, the client utters it for herself. I must also gain the confidence to remain unknowing, to have a sense of 'being adrift' (Ogden, 1999):

> . . . Negative Capability, that is, when a man is capable of being in uncertainties, mysteries, doubts, without any irritable reaching after fact and reason. (Keats, 1817, cited in Rollins, 1958)

Witnessing

It is for us an absolute rule always to believe the client's story, and to be able to recognize and acknowledge the validity of the experience recounted, however distant and 'other' to one's own; to be open to the experience and to allow it to permeate one's being. 'Empathy' can be such an insult, when confronted by the extremities of what humans can survive. And in the obverse, in a situation where a client is aware of being privileged in some fashion, and that her own suffering in relation to the extremes may seem slight, to remain aware that nevertheless we all suffer our own torments in our own unique way.

Part of witnessing is to stand forth and name what it is that is being described in its full horror – to use the word 'rape', to use the word 'death', to use the word 'terror', when the style of the discourse is designed to hide from or to baffle, when clients may not have dared to name, or when the significance or reality of a situation requires, in the name of justice, to be inscribed on the lips and hearts of the two who know.

Meeting

H: The term 'dialogue' is often imbued with a degree of import, is rarified in some way; is seen as some sort of quest. I think it's simply a quest for genuine meeting, which is rare enough in itself, and potentially so powerful so that something of truth emerges in that moment. Having grander goals is not necessary; in fact, I'm not sure what a grander goal would be.

> Meeting on the other hand can be seen as a culmination. The Thou meets me through grace – it is not found by seeking. But my speaking of the primary word to it is an

act of my being, is indeed the act of my being. (Buber, 1958: 24, cited in Goldenberg and Isaacson, 1996: 121)

Being-with-the-Other

… it was as though the element of vitality itself bordered on my skin, something that was not I, was certainly not akin to me, palpably the other, not just another, really the Other itself; and yet it let me approach, confided itself to me, placed itself elementally in the relation of *Thou* and *Thou* with me. (Buber, 1965: 22–3)

To demonstrate a willingness, a preparedness to go from one's self towards another; to make the leap to another vision, recognizing that we all have different visions. To encompass another vision within your scheme of things, within yourself, alongside your own, and to allow the two to impact on each other and bring something new out of that. It is precisely at these rare moments of genuine, full, uncalculated 'being to being' meeting that therapy, or for that matter teaching/learning, takes place.

Knowing

If I don't know that I don't know I think I know and if I don't know that I know I think I don't know. (Laing, 1970: 55)

Yet always I must remember that there is danger in thinking that I know: it is difficult to see how I as therapist, standing forth, inevitably, as a representative of an esoteric elite within the perspective of the western value-system, and who is approached by prospective clients as the one (of the therapeutic dyad) who knows, who has been initiated into knowing within this cultural context, can avoid imposing this set of values on their clients, despite whatever my best intentions may be to refrain from doing so. This confidential and 'clandestine' relationship also presents the opportunity for the therapist, in being the one who knows about the Other, to avoid and escape from her own 'unknowingness', into the task of 'helping' the Other.

Arlow (1993) speaks of a process whereby alongside the empathy arises intuitive processing through which the therapist's inner experience and introspection are organized, transformed into insight.

> Feeling and thinking transform apparently the therapist's
> random associations or disconnected thoughts at times
> into a coherent hypothesis. Theoretical knowledge acts as
> a base for the embodiment of experiential knowledge –
> the internalisation of the analytic person and process.
> Embodied knowledge is partial in that it is about living
> within the limits and contradictions of our own ability to
> experience. (Arlow, 1993, cited in Gardner, 1995: 433)

Unknowing

... 'un-knowing' refers to that attempt to remain as open as possible to whatever presents itself to our relational experience. As such, it expresses the attempt to treat the seemingly familiar, or that of which we are either aware or informed, as novel, unfixed in meaning, accessible to previously unexamined possibilities. (Spinelli, 1997: 8)

> Bion ... enjoined therapists to approach sessions 'without
> memory or desire ... Discard your memory, discard the

future tense of your desire; forget them both, both what you knew and what you want, to leave space for a new idea. A thought, an idea unchained, may be floating around the room searching for a home. Amongst these may be one of your own which seems to turn up from your insides, or one from outside yourself, namely the patient ... (Gordon, 1999: 89/90)

A student commented that: 'the course represents for me the continuing rehabilitation of the mind and of thinking, counter-balancing the amount of my training which was "humanistic", with its emphasis on "feeling". Paradoxically, as my ability to grasp various theoretical perspectives grows, I find myself much more at ease with "NOT knowing"' (Stanton, 1993: 235–6).

Thinking

A therapist is not working unless she is thinking, or allowing her internal 'participant observer' to continue that work, and to be able to access this from time to time. But thinking is also the capacity to hold the Other 'in mind', to act as a container for the anxiety, acknowledged, or more often unacknowledged, which prevents or paralyses the thinking of the Other.

Initially I should be able to 'taste' the main streams of theorizing, as I would engage in a wine-tasting. Theories and ideas should be taught as far as possible 'from the inside', in such a way that learners have a real opportunity 'to try on for size' a range of ways of thinking about the dilemmas inherent in being human and a chance to think for themselves about the thoughts of others. (Ideas in the field of psychotherapy should be accompanied by a health warning, since some teachers are inclined to present, and some learners to receive, the ideas of The Master as a revelation, rather than a hypothesis!) In the service of working towards 'embodied knowing' I should have the opportunity, through experiential exercises in pairs, small groups, or other variations of the class group, to allow myself and my personal experience to be questioned by the explorations and conclusions of others, and, of course, *vice versa.*

As I progress through the training process I shall expect to explore these ideas further, with whatever lesser streams or topics of 'thinking about' arise out of my own personal inclinations, interests, personal experience, intended area of particular professional focus.

H: As we're thinking about the tendency to fall into a 'pure' intellectual approach, the question of the mind/body split arises. A student said, 'I agree entirely that it is an artificial split but it is so embedded in our culture, and it is so hard to approach it in a different way.' I said, 'Yes, but it's possible.' I asked, 'What's your own experience of this? Do you experience your mind and body as two separate entities?'

If you wanted to identify a handful of fundamental things that cause us pain or that we bring to therapy, one of those would be that we doubt our own sense of reality. So we know that as teachers with our own vulnerabilities and blind spots it's all too easy to collude in some way with that desire for an answer to exist somewhere out there, however much we claim to be offering a spectrum of possibilities, and saying: 'See what resonates for you.'

M: Why would it resonate unless – it might be just one word or phrase – something is recognized? If I recognize, it is because I have experienced it, but haven't been able to either conceptualize, or to actually notice or really experience, because of a lack of language.

Reading

M: I hear myself say very frequently, 'Stick to the required reading list. Try this book – it's on the list; you should read it.' But by 'reading' I mean 'sit with it, look at the contents, look at a few chapters; if this book or author is not speaking to you in an active way, then put it down, because you two are not meant to meet'. It's a pointless exercise to think you have to sit down and read the book from start to finish because it's on the required reading list; it might be a theoretical perspective that is meaningless to you; either it's not right for you, full stop; or it's not right for you now. Perhaps later, perhaps not, it might mean something to you. What is the point of engaging or attempting to engage with a text if there is no answer from you to what is being spoken by the text?

H: That gives responsibility back to the reader – required reading or not; asking students to notice their own experience, their own reaction, to question a sense of discomfort on reading (or not reading) a particular text.

The question of dialogue with the text arises, which takes me to the style of studying *Talmud*. People say that's not really dialogue, because text is a flat thing, but in fact it's somebody's creation, and in that sense is very much a living, organic entity.

M: It's an encounter between the reader and the text and what arises out of that ...

H: ... which itself is a lived experience. Interestingly I must add, that *Talmud* is always studied in pairs. It's the idea that the whole is greater than the sum of the parts – I have my encounter with the text, you have your encounter with the text, but out of our

125

exchange something more emerges. There is, of course, a parallel with our conversation this very moment, and with our collaboration in the writing of this book. We are not attempting to speak as a singular voice, or to offer a singular 'truth'.

'Skills' Practice

Equally fundamental to learning is the capacity to be open to critical feedback derived from direct observation of an interaction that takes place in the context of a small group made up of fellow students and teacher – respectfully offered additional and/or alternative perspectives on the interaction between speaker and listener, who involve themselves in the roles of therapist and client. An essential feature for us of all early 'practical' training is that participants have a real possibility of meeting each other, rather than being encouraged to act the part of a therapist or client. The setting of the interaction may be artificial, in that participants are thrown together in a public classroom environment rather than freely choosing to meet each other in a confidential professional consulting room, yet the aim is to allow participants to find the truth in each encounter, whatever the 'initial conditions'. They are not encouraged to ignore the training environment, but to work with the givens and to make every effort to be present in the actuality of the 'now'.

The work in what we call 'triads' (each member of a group of three taking turns to function as 'listener', 'client', 'observer') presents an unparalleled opportunity to test out the nature of this encounter. It is vital that neither of the active participants fully slip into the role of 'client' and 'therapist', that they remain firmly in the 'now', yet, as listeners become (hopefully) more at ease, more still within themselves, more attentive to the other, the quality of the 'being-together' will itself affirm the 'being-ness' of the speaker.

126

The observer acts as a second listener, 'a silent listener'. While the observer generally feels himself to be under less pressure, whether from the evaluation required by the course or merely from fact of being under scrutiny, and so may feel more 'free', more non-participant, the task of observation is a crucial one. The feedback given by an observer who is a witness to the encounter (and therefore influences it), when this is carefully thought through and judiciously presented, can be unrepeatably valuable to the listener. This will echo the value of supervision, and, indeed, is closely related; but these 'practice sessions' offer a unique possibility of 'live' observation that simply cannot take place with 'real clients' without fatally compromising the therapeutic intention.

Reflection

The concept of 'reverie' is often attributed to psychoanalysis, yet all therapists would recognize that

> the emotional disturbances associated with reverie regularly feel ... a product of [one's] own interfering preoccupations, excessive narcissistic self-absorption, immaturity, unresolved emotional conflicts, and so on. The ... difficulty in making use of his reveries in the service of analysis is easily understandable since such experience is usually so close, so immediate, that it is difficult to see: it is 'too present to imagine'. (Ogden, 1999: 163)

Reflection, with others, on the interaction just witnessed, gives a rare 'third eye' on the experience of an intersubjective reverie.

Self-reflection

The capacity to reflect upon and question ourselves is what makes humans distinct from other living creatures. An essential part of training is the continual, unremitting encouragement of the ability and willingness to reflect upon one's actions, motivations, sensations, values, to name but a few.

It is through such activities as we have described above that I (the reflective 'I') learn how to take a (relatively) objective stance in relation to my actions/words. If it is difficult for me to discern matters and motives which lie outside of my awareness, the presence and the input from a third 'I' will assist me in allowing a connection to be made between my undisclosed emotions and my active cognition, delivering 'insight'.

Understanding

> Wifred Bion is reported to have commented to his analysand, James Grotstein, after Grotstein responded to one of Bion's interpretations with 'I understand': 'Please try not to understand. If you must, superstand, circumstand, parastand, but please try not to understand'. (Personal communication, cited in Ogden, 1999: 208)

The quest for understanding may become one of the losses for the trainee therapist. Making that leap from seeking 'knowledge and understanding' to being able to tolerate the 'not knowing' is a critical step in the process from trainee to practitioner – one that, in fact, remains to be grappled with always.

Being-with-Others

Being-with-others is a constant, yet takes on different shapes throughout a training day. The final (usually, in the scheme of the day) element in all psychotherapy training is the challenge of not only surviving, but being able to make use of, the arena of the process group – a small group of peers together with a 'facilitator', as a forum for exploration of individual and interpersonal process in relation to the course. This may mean exploration in some respects analogous to therapy or to group therapy, a process that is limited, constrained and balanced as the individual member and the group decide(s), with the monitoring and sometimes guiding presence of the group facilitator. The group experience parallels that of life, with its 'thrownness' into a set of givens. The group membership is not chosen, but created through the more or less random procedure of membership of the course, and the group has no explicit agenda other than to explore the nature of being-together in this context.

In any group, it will be the random, throw-away remark, the casual greeting, that can denote or trigger an issue which holds significance for the group as a whole and learning – sometimes hard and painful – for individual group members. The group facilitator must be prepared to ensure that such difficulties generate and become the learning, moderating or 'containing' conflict or bringing out opposite and/or minority views as necessary.

To increase our ability to openly examine personal, professional and interpersonal issues is a crucial part of training. Acknowledging, addressing, and seeking to find a way to be-with conflict and difference within the group context can expose the tension, fear or even terror that underlie our attempts to be-with each other – to belong to and yet not be engulfed by the group itself.

The group is the real-life arena where we play or act out the learning/unlearning of the day. Difficulties and shortcomings invisible elsewhere reveal themselves in what can sometimes be the 'cauldron' of the group. Tutor and students alike must accept responsibility for the tensions that inevitably arise from the particular chemistry evolving in each group, and be willing to explore, however tentatively, the ensuing process.

Yet the process group also offers an important learning about a change of rhythm, pace and balance in my way of being-with, and about the challenge that this arena poses to my sense of myself, to my self-and-environment-constructed identity. What may constitute a 'safe-enough' environment in which to allow and facilitate such necessary challenge, must be discovered and explored afresh by every different group, by every unique group facilitator. Without such an opportunity, such a challenge, each learner can fail to be confronted with her impact on the Other (group members) which foreshadows and prefigures her impact on future clients.

Getting into my Stride: Clinical Placement

A key element of all training is the clinical work, through which the novice practitioner becomes an autonomous psychotherapist or counsellor. Training psychotherapists are required to seek out and negotiate an opportunity to work with clients in a setting which provides a 'safe-enough' environment for the work with clients. Until that arena is entered, all learning is 'theoretical', or provisional.

Each specific placement organization will be different, usually outside the direct control of the training organization. The relationship between trainee and placement is based on mutual exchange: the trainee therapist is offering time and growing expertise and in return is gaining experience of the work and, normally, supervision. Each trainee will develop her own unique way of dealing with the 'housekeeping' aspects of the work, policies and procedures regarding not only lines of management and clinical responsibility, guidelines and procedures relating to ethical issues, including complaints procedures, but also the day-to-day problems that present themselves as 'mere' practicalities, but which form the bread-and-butter experience of therapy for the client and which represent the dilemmas and lived reality of therapy. All of these constitute the 'frame' for the work, for which each therapist must consider herself responsible, despite her novice status, since it shapes and influences the interaction in many unforeseen ways.

Supervision

Supervision is an essential and ongoing element of that safe environment, the 'secure base' from which the 'young' therapist goes out, and to which she returns as a source of support and energy (this applies to experienced practitioners as well as trainees). The supervisor also provides 'insurance' for the clients of learning therapists, mitigating the clandestine nature of the therapeutic relationship and acting as an advocate for the client, while supporting the practitioner in her ceaseless struggle to be-with her clients. The supervisory relationship, at its best, also provides a model as an arena for the discipline of lifelong learning.

It is useful during training to have supervision from more than one perspective. No single perspective can claim to be the 'truth' of any given interaction, so it is valuable for competing interpretations of the nature of the interaction to be exposed so that areas of interface and divergence can be considered and clarified. The inevitable resulting tension caused by contrasting and potentially even contradictory ideas about the nature and dynamics of any particular interaction fosters a paradoxical security in the practitioner who has to learn to tolerate ambiguity and the absence of a fixed truth. In any case, such an experience allows a 'young' psychotherapist to grow into her own chosen way of being-with clients.

Training supervision is an opportunity to reflect with others in an intimate, yet public forum on the interaction with clients. Attention in this context builds on the prior learning from triad work, focusing on the therapeutic alliance established; the recognition and acknowledgement of recurring themes in the client's current and past significant relationships; the significance of therapeutic boundaries and how their disturbance may affect the therapeutic relationship; the rationale for and formulation of interventions, the recognition of personal issues that may be evoked for therapists by client's material; the capacity to sit in silence with clients, and to manage breaks and endings. Equally, trainees should be able to learn to make use of supervision to enhance their personal, clinical and professional development. A willingness to acknowledge the social realities of clients' lives is also vital; for many clients have the experience of exclusion or discrimination, in one form or another, in ways that powerfully shape their experience and their sense of themselves. Nor is the therapeutic relationship itself immune from institutionalized biases and prejudices.

The supervisor carries a degree of responsibility for the practice of her supervisee, and in the context of training this includes the responsibility to evaluate the trainee's progress in relation to clinical work. Training supervisors and trainees engage in a process of dialogue delineating and, to some extent, measuring progress. Without dialogue on both sides of this interaction there can be little learning. Supervision in small groups also enhances the aspect of dialogue and interaction with peers, which furthers the learning, although this depends on the learner working through the experience of shame engendered by this 'public' disclosure of shortcomings and 'failures' in relation to her work with the client.

Writing

Writing is an instrument of learning: a facilitative process of articulating thoughts, setting down an account, whether of an episode or session in a therapeutic interaction, or of a developing thread of reflection on an event or an idea. In a collaborative interaction with marks on a page, one sees and thus does thinking. The discipline of seeking to make one's thinking clear and comprehensible to another must always be a valuable one. Writing in the professional/clinical sphere also sets the task of managing to discuss with clarity work with colleagues or clients in a way that nevertheless respects their privacy and preserves the confidentiality of their 'material'.

If I can write about a topic, developing a critical under-standing of, searching out the weaknesses in, developing my own thinking through this exercise, I expand and complexify my mental capacities, languages and insight into the dilemmas of being human.

The more I seek to clarify and unearth the kernel of the matter for the learning and scrutiny of others, the more I enlarge my own understanding. Essays, client studies, an extended piece of writing such as a dissertation, all entail learning the meaning of thinking, and of research, finding ways of submitting a theory to the test of examination or exploration.

Process Reports and Client Studies

A process report is essentially a brief record of and reflection on one or more sessions with a client, including the interactive and dynamic process of the interaction, exploration of the therapist's contributions and later reflection on the experience of supervision. It may also include discussion of challenging moments and an overview of the therapist's holistic responses during the session.

Such writing is focused on developing understanding of my interaction with the client, reflecting the collaborative process of making meaning in the therapeutic experience. It also articulates and facilitates my reflection on and learning through the collaborative supervisory dialogue.

This also applies to client (case) studies.[1] The study should present an overview of my work with a client and should include description of the setting and arrangements which form the 'initial conditions' shaping the work, as well as some narrative describing how the interaction unfolded, alongside my self-reflection. I should try to show how I 'kept the client in mind'; what difficulties and challenges we encountered and how I sought to address these. I should include consideration of alternative approaches or possible ways of understanding the interaction, and an exploration of the ethical dilemmas posed by this unique interaction.

Personal Development Essays

There is an art to writing about oneself in the context of an academic and professional training of this kind, in which (we cannot too often reiterate) the personal *is* the professional. Again, such a task presents an opportunity for (yet another) form of therapy, as I set down a narrative of my learning about myself, about myself-with-other, and about myself-as-practitioner. I learn to reflect on my actions, on my behaviour, as these are

---

1. The expression 'case study' serves to de-humanize, medicalize and objectify the individual designated as a 'case'.

impacted upon by my interaction with the diverse others whom I meet in this environment. I seek to find a balance, a consensus, between my feeling, my thinking, and my actions, setting these down in a fashion that can be 'read' by another, and this articulation, this coming together of experience and self-reflection in the presence of a reader, will constitute my progress.

Research

All human knowledge is provisional: we are all researchers, inquirers, investigators of the many facets of what it means to be in the world. My perspective, my opinion, is bounded and distorted by my limitations as a subject. There will always be a core of therapeutic practice which research can never directly touch, yet in order to monitor my experience and my practice I need systematically to reflect with others; I need to be in dialogue with 'the distilled knowledge generated by systematic reflection and analysis of the practice of many ...' (McLeod, 2001: 3).

Progress in understanding the 'what' and the 'how' of psychotherapy can only develop out of practice: there is no 'laboratory' other than the consulting-room. Research can be helpful in reconstructing practice, and we are confident that it will support a pluralistic conception of therapy. The critical dilemmas in living reported by a range of individual clients should be represented, together with the diversity and complexity of possible responses and interventions. This would reaffirm the legitimacy of the activity in the eyes of its stakeholders, and would offer valuable opportunities for continuing learning for the practitioner, as well as for a wider audience about what it means to be human in this particular social context. Each unique encounter, each unique client, and client-with-therapist, can never be 'reduced' to a research project, yet 'science' – the sum of provisional human knowledge – has evolved through the opening up and setting forth of an individual's experience for 'peer review' and the critique and analysis of others.

There are methodologies that are more and less suited to research in this arena: 'there is certainly an important role to be played by traditional forms of research … But there is also a vital role for emerging forms of research that are qualitative, experiential, narrative and case-based' and that allow 'multi-voiced' pluralism and inclusiveness (*ibid*: 10), as well as explicitly acknowledging the impact of the researcher herself. A clear rationale for the design and methodology adopted by researchers should establish how such a study could be useful, to further understanding either of the therapeutic endeavour itself or of human development and experience more generally.

Respect for and protection of participants (co-researchers) must be paramount. The ethics of research must be explicitly and systematically addressed in training, in relation to the protection of clients' privacy and the confidentiality of their material: serious and careful consideration must be given to the specific meaning for each participant of 'informed consent'. As an example, the impact on both client and therapist of the technology of audio- and video-recording of sessions must be closely investigated and monitored – a discipline which undertakes to explore hidden and underlying concerns and dynamics cannot afford to adopt a superficial assumption in seeking co-researchers' consent that 'Yes' necessarily means 'Yes', or that the quest for 'evidence' necessarily outranks other considerations. Further, publication of client study material has ramifications relating to respect for the 'ownership' of material and the experience, ideas and feelings 'donated' by participant clients, which might be construed as a kind of 'mind-theft' (a student's term), rather than legitimate research 'data' (as we have discovered from diligent detective work, for example, on Freud's patients).

Dissertation

An extended piece of work which incorporates and seeks to 'integrate' personal experience, theoretical exploration, and some aspect of clinical practice or other 'application' presents a significant developmental task. The preparation of a dissertation can constitute a synthesizing process; the mantra: 'the personal is the professional' indicates that there will be radical differences in the ways that different individuals approach this exercise. For many, it may be almost entirely an academic exercise, with the personal excluded in favour of a model based on the empirical research study. For others, the creative process constitutes a profoundly personal understanding which encapsulates the whole life struggle, the whole pattern thus far, so that the finished piece of work represents an extremely significant point in personal development.

In relation to the quality of an extended piece of writing, much depends on the 'success' of the collaboration known as 'academic supervision'. At best this can be the most exciting one-to-one activity that takes place between teacher and learner, where one can see the development occurring through a process of carefully calibrated attunement. The experience, whether of being on the 'giving' or the 'receiving' end of such a facilitative activity, is rewarding precisely because the teacher learns from the learner, and the learner feels enabled and affirmed in his autonomous development as a psychotherapist, scholar and/or clinician. The more the individual can recognize the usefulness of the exercise, the more fully he can be aware of his personal engagement, the more he can be perceived to be reaching down into the depth of the self to actually produce the words on the page. Many dissertations are written not only in the sweat of the brow, but in blood and tears ...

Evaluation

The process of evaluation in the field of psychotherapy training should be analogous to a masterclass in music. Not that the one who evaluates is a master of the art, but that the skills of observation and feedback should be highly tuned in the service of a dialogue of 'playing' and critique/instruction/commendation. This should apply in respect of whatever the aspect being evaluated. Yet the evaluator must not flinch from exercising judgement, so that a grade can be given – always, however, on the basis that the rationale for the grade is clear, that the criteria are known beforehand, and that the subjectivity of the one evaluator may be balanced by an alternative perspective of another evaluator, in order that a final, overall judgement becomes a matter of a consensus of subjectivity. The giving of a grade is, in itself, a gift (sometimes an unwelcome one!): it provides clear and specific feedback, against a set of criteria, which will enable a learner later to fine-tune his 'performance'.

All of this is to some extent captured in the phrase in current use describing the desired model of 'the Reflective Practitioner': ideas and theories regarding the process and vicissitudes of human development, engaged with and subjected to the test of personal experience and reflection; the practice of 'being-with' in ways that can be reflected on with others; and the group as the forum for a 'public' reflection on a process of differentiated learning, the whole programme encouraging the involvement of the whole person within an environment whose boundaries in time, pacing, privacy and confidentiality are carefully managed.

The more we know, the more we recognize how much we don't know. There is, and should continue to be, a necessary tension between the 'teaching' of ways of being, which involve the development of an ability and willingness to be at a place of un-knowing, and the 'teaching' of theory, which becomes a valuable 'knowledge-base' to refer to when making those in-the-moment decisions in the confines of the consulting room.

Failure to Learn/Teach

H: There is a shared process between therapists, clients and teachers; ultimately for each of us it is terrifying to be-with the 'not-knowing' or to acknowledge uncertainty. A combination of tolerance of uncertainty, with a deep inquisitiveness, is what we are attempting to cultivate. As teachers, part of what we should be trying to model is a degree of, not necessarily comfort, but preparedness, to tolerate 'not knowing', and to resist the temptation to 'know'.

M: It's a big thing for students to place their confidence in a tutor, and in a training organization. They trust that we know what we are about, and may assume that this will mean they are going to get a piece of paper, an award, a qualification, through trusting themselves to the organization. We therefore have to be prepared for that sharp conflict, the terrible difficulties we have around the failure of the process, when something goes wrong and the judgement is of failure. Then we, the tutor, the organization, are accused of or are shown to have failed, and we must explore this failure. We are in the 'business' of training: we claim: 'We can make you a therapist'; we put out for sale the process that we all trust will end with a piece of paper, a 'qualification'. There is conflict between selling a service, maintaining the viability of the training organization, and serving the best interests both of the students who entrust themselves to us and also of their future clients.

H: Students are entitled to an early warning of possible failure. As therapists we often find it difficult to make assessments, believing as we do that people always have the potentiality to develop; we've used this as a cop-out in the past. I think what often happens is that there is something problematic that doesn't get confronted by the teacher, doesn't get brought out into the open. I'm sure that's not the case in all incidents, but it's that aspect of confrontation that's so difficult and that gets passed on … By the end, when it becomes unavoidable, there may be a sense of urgency; but by then it may also be too late in the process, for it raises the question for the student, 'So what's been going on all this time?'.

M: Yes, and that's often expressed quite directly, the difficulty being something about the subjectivity of this – 'Is this just me; is this just my difficulty, or is it just between us?'. Or is it a real lack, or problem, of the student, in which case the institution or the teacher has to take responsibility for saying to the student, 'Unless you do so and so, you will not pass, you will not qualify, etc.', and that's a really hard thing to say. It's harder because it may be a very difficult thing to put into concrete terms. That's why to some extent we dodge it; we seek to avoid the task of showing, with justice and clarity and fairness, what it is that somebody is failing to do, and what they will be required to do in order to move from a 'fail' judgement to a 'pass' judgement.

H: I had the experience of working with a supervisee who had received a critical evaluation prior to our working together. I felt her approach to be very muddled. It was an uphill task, but we had one session together in which we both made enormous efforts to engage with her confusion. She kept coming back to me, saying: 'I don't understand. What should I be doing? What is the difference between what I am doing, and what I should be doing?'. She was quite insistent. I had to call on quite a lot of resources, thinking carefully about language; I was exhausted by the end of the hour (I suspect she was too), but we worked at it together. It was incredibly gratifying, took an enormous effort, a leap of awareness and understanding in the student. She could see there was a problem, but not actually what the problem was ...

M: Then the two of you together have a problem.

H: There seemed to be such a parallel with therapy. Even when a client may be in an extreme state she may feel quite safe if she can sense that I am really trying to make that leap into her logic. There is a logic: our challenge is: 'How can I get the thread of this logic? It's not my logic, but I must decode this.' The satisfaction that I felt was to do with: 'I'm trying, I'm really trying.'

M: We all have particular skills, and I was recently most impressed by a colleague in a difficult situation. I'm afraid I was taking a relatively hostile position; I wanted to say to this particular student, 'What are you about in all of this? How does your (bad) behaviour relate to the fact that you are trying to become a therapist?'. I was in that 'shock, horror, blame' mode, and my colleague did a great job of stepping back from all of that, and trying to show, or explain, the concern, and to meet the student in a way that allowed this person to begin to see what the difficulty was. It was quite exceptional, and very educational for me.

Personal Therapy

Personal experience of therapy is essential to learning to become a therapist. While we would strenuously contest the idea that all therapy is 'good', or that psychotherapy constitutes the only 'path to enlightenment' (or whatever), if I have not been on the 'receiving end' of both 'good' and 'bad' therapeutic experiences, I will be the less able to envisage possible effects of my behaviour on the other.

To propose that I do not 'need' therapy is to feel comfortable with my lack of awareness of how my own 'woundedness' will always be implicated in my way of being-with. Such a stance shows, at best, a lack of curiosity about my own processes, and a lack of awareness that not only am I never fully what I can be, but I am never fully aware of what I am.

Conversely, therapy that is undertaken merely in order to meet the requirements of a training is likely to be a travesty, as may be, in some respects, the practice known as a 'training analysis'. In both cases there cannot but be a divided and therefore ambivalent agenda, which is likely, in various subtle and undetectable ways, to deflect attention and energy away from 'the client' and towards 'his (prospective) clients'.

We would hope that some applicants for training will have made the decision to seek training 'out of', so to speak, a 'good' therapeutic experience, so that they will thus feel the discipline to be an honourable undertaking. Those that may seek training 'out of' a negative or mediocre experience of therapy may be doing so in an attempt either to prove themselves a better therapist, or as a means of 'getting even'! (The 'wrong' reasons for coming to training do not necessarily invalidate the project.)

We would not necessarily insist that applicants for training have, as an entry requirement, had, or be having, experience as a client. We have found it to be clearly advantageous to learners, acting as a significant 'booster' – an additional dimension – to initial learning. But, since psychotherapy is by no means necessarily either the 'only' or the 'best' route to self-development/self-awareness/personal maturity, we see disadvantage, discrimination and exclusiveness in such a demand.

Ongoing personal therapy throughout training, however, is necessary and vital, offering an additional means of personal support through an intensely 'affective' learning process, as well as an alternative project of self-exploration that is parallel to, extends and deepens the learning in the arena of training. It is also a crucial self-indulgence or luxury, being (we trust) a place for unbridled 'being-for-myself', a very necessary antidote to all this 'being-for-another'!

The whole of the training is greater than the sum of its parts: all of these diverse activities together do not in and of themselves constitute a training, but they, together with the unique person of the individual trainee, her interaction with her colleagues and tutors, her individual past and ongoing life experience, external to the training, and events in the social and political context in which the training unfolds, come together to contribute to a process of possible metamorphosis.

6
An Ethical Endeavour

If I am not for myself who will be for me, but if I am
only for myself what am I, and if not now, when?
(Hillel)

We are always, as our existential forebears remind us, '... in-the-
world' (Binswanger, 1963; Heidegger, 1962, 1977) – how we are
in the world is the ethical dimension. Ethics, the value base
which informs all one's actions in the world, with the
environment and with its creatures, animal and human, forms
the essential backdrop to the practice of psychotherapy and the
training of psychotherapists.

So we must ask: 'What does it mean to encounter another
human being?' 'What is the meaning of my responsibility to that
other?' No psychotherapist can avoid these questions, which are
fundamental to the psychotherapeutic endeavour. No one has
posed these questions more radically, or more intransigently, and
no one has suggested answers more radical than the
French–Jewish philosopher Emmanual Levinas. Levinas placed
ethics at the heart of philosophy. In particular, he argued that
ethics is responsibility for the Other, that this responsibility
precedes knowledge and, moreover, has nothing whatsoever to
do with reciprocity, that is I do not do something in order to get
something in return. Furthermore, Levinas argued, it is this

ethical responsibility which constitutes me as a subject, it is the meaning of my subjectivity.

Ethics understood in this way is at the heart of psychotherapy, and demands that we abandon a great many preconceptions and assumptions about our relations with others. I offer and present myself to the Other and accept the opportunity to meet with the Other in his wholeness as a person with a radical openness towards his 'strangeness' which avoids reducing the Other to what is already known to us.

The ethical values which underlie and are articulated in the actions of both teachers and practitioners of psychotherapy should broadly encompass notions of respect for persons, individual autonomy, confidence in the human capacity for self-directed change, and a willingness to shoulder responsibility for one's own behaviour. Such a stance is at odds with anything resembling an 'expert' model of practice or training. It also counters the perspective which sees in the Other only a version of myself, a view which appropriates the Other through some assumed knowledge or claimed understanding.

Tillich defines ethics as the science of man's mortal existence, the roots of the moral imperative, the criterion by which the validity of existence is evaluated. There is no answer in ethics without an explicit or implicit assertion about the nature of being (Tillich, 1960: 72), a claim of some magnitude.

The reader will have noticed a subtle debate permeating this book. On the one hand, we speak of asymmetry of power and responsibility, yet, on the other, speak of reciprocity and mutuality in the therapeutic relationship. Levinas speaks of the asymmetry of my relations towards the Other, which we understand to refer to my obligation towards the Other, independent of any expectation of reciprocity (Am I my brother's keeper? Yes); in addition we highlight the asymmetry of the therapist/client dyad, emphasizing the imbalance of power between therapist and client, and the onus put upon the therapist therefore to behave with restraint. Yet at the same time, we remind readers that the therapist as well as the client comes away affected by the encounter. Buber points out that in fact 'relation' – the *a priori* of existence – offers the possibility of a rhythmic 'mutuality' between myself and the Other.

> Dialogue is a reciprocal process of address and response. A dialogic relation is one founded upon an openness to the other based on an attitude of You-saying, that is of one subject to another, and an acceptance of my responsibility to be responsive to the other. The life of dialogue is a life of mutuality, lived in immediacy (i.e. direct, not mediated) and the polar opposite of an alienated existence. (Buber, cited in Goldenberg and Isaacson, 1996: 126–7)

That relation must be based on and rendered mutual through the continuous and deliberate examination (by both therapist and client) of the ethical values we have proposed.

The Question of Power

> In any encounter of man with man, power is active, the power of the personal radiation, expressed in language and gestures, in the glance of the eye and the sound of the voice, in face and figure and movement, expressed in what one is personally and what one represents socially. Every encounter, whether friendly or hostile, whether benevolent or indifferent, is in some way, unconsciously or consciously, a struggle of power with power. (Tillich, 1960: 87)

Power, fear, inequality, abuse – all too frequently these words seem to go together. On the face of it we have greater autonomy, freedom, and 'rights' than ever before in human history, and yet we fear for our physical and personal safety and integrity to as great a degree as ever before. A. C. Grayling, (*Guardian*, 11 May 2002) speaks of 'might': 'the tragic fact that whenever individuals ... become powerful, they apply the crude and ancient principle that might is right, and concomitantly refuse to subordinate their power to wider and higher laws. The possession of unlimited power will make a despot of almost any man. There is a possible Nero in the gentlest creature that walks.' Grayling argues that 'the only restraint on the tendency of power to debase its holder ... is a structure of law, with proper methods and independent judges' (Grayling, 2002).

We are arguing that such a structure, while necessary, is not enough. A more proactive understanding is required as a way of ordering the 'clandestine' interaction between therapist and client, while ultimately the therapist remains alone with her conscience, 'on her honour'. And so, a private, internalized form of restraint is suggested by Shakespeare's *King Lear*, a work of uncompromising bleakness, charting Lear's journey through madness to a modicum of self-awareness, which

> ... emerges in the struggle with madness which is the
> process ... of the reordering, the restructuring of his
> inner world, in order for him to acknowledge his own
> part in, and responsibility for, human evil, hypocrisy and
> injustice. Lear's madness ... is ... a metaphor for the
> struggle of humanity to come to terms with its existence
> in the world, and for the struggle to determine the values
> by which that existence is to be regulated ... Through his
> madness, Lear achieves a restored imagination ...
> (Sullivan, 1995: 89)

A 'restored imagination' which allows us to stand in the shoes of the Other is a means to allow the power of the therapist to be recognized and acknowledged before it can be restrained so that the power of the client has the opportunity to be realized.

We are tentatively suggesting that therapists have a personal agenda related to making reparation and to acting out of love in this particular fashion, which may also be a way of dealing with the frustrations and sufferings of our past. Such a form of love, since it informs and drives such an undertaking, must be constantly monitored and tested.

According to Paul Tillich, love, power and justice are woven together with a golden thread:

> Each of the three concepts in itself and all three in relation to each other are universally significant: they appear in decisive places in the doctrine of man, in psychology and jurisprudence, they determine political theory and educational method, they cannot be avoided even in mental and bodily medicine. (Tillich, 1960: 1)

He maintains that love and justice are interdependent in any interaction between persons. What he calls 'forgiving love' is, he claims, the only way of fulfilling the intrinsic claim in every being, namely its claim to be reaccepted into the unity of the human community to which she belongs, yet from which she is excluded through her suffering. Such love, enacted through being present to the pain articulated by clients, exposes and acknowledges the break with justice effected by their experience, and in the witnessing thereof, allows and co-creates a reparative 'validation' of their truth.

However, in any ethical discourse love alone is not enough: love does not eliminate the need for justice: we do not escape the responsibility and the self-restraint demanded by justice by claiming to act out of love. An ethical interpersonal endeavour must be recognizable as an enactment of 'natural justice', which Tillich (1960) represents as the (true) form of being. (Pain, damage, hurt are but forms of non-being which contravene the 'ought-ness' of 'is'.) He maintains that the 'Golden Rule' ('Do unto others as you would have them do unto you') is not enough: 'we are suspicious of others as we would be of ourselves; we suspect that behind the manifest meaning of the demand something else is hidden that should be rejected, an unconscious hostility, the desire to dominate, the will to exploit, the instinct of self-destruction' (*ibid*: 79).

The emphasis on neutrality and distance in the practice of psychotherapy, particularly within the psychoanalytic paradigm, accentuates (in part, creates) the power asymmetries present in the therapeutic encounter. The therapist remains mysterious while the client discloses his most intimate recesses; the therapist is silent while the client speaks; the client is observed, the therapist invisible; everything the client says is scrutinized for hidden meanings. The therapist's utterances carry immense weight, and the therapist, assumed always to be working in the best interests of the client and from the best intentions, can never be confronted.

On the other hand, power is a life force. While we remain cowed by its potentiality and focus on all its dangerous aspects, we give all too little attention to our personal power; we have not become familiar with it, discovered its ambit, cultivated its hue and shape. In the face of might we abdicate. It is easier, less daunting, less onerous than staking our claim on existence.

> Our deepest fear is not that we are inadequate, our
> deepest fear is that we are powerful beyond measure. It is
> our light not our darkness that most frightens us.
> We ask ourselves, 'Who am I to be brilliant, gorgeous,
> talented, fabulous?'

Actually who are you not to be? You are a child of God.
Your playing small doesn't serve the world. There's
nothing enlightened about shrinking so that other people
won't feel insecure around you. We are meant to shine as
children do. We were born to make manifest the glory of
God that is within us and it's not just within some of us,
it's in everyone. And as we let our own light shine we
unconsciously give other people permission to do the
same. As we're liberated from our own fear our presence
automatically liberates others. (Mandela, 1994)

We recognize the presence of each of us in the world as a potential
powerful force, our interconnection with all the elements of the
world, and our individual obligation towards the world.

In choosing the particular path of therapy one is owning the
potentiality of what it is for two people to sit with each other. We
are owning the fact that our presence (or the lack of it) may have
an impact on the Other and that that impact may resonate
throughout their world. We are acknowledging that we are quiet
activists sowing seeds at the micro level, that may permeate out
into the world at large. We see a glimpse of our power and own
it as our ethical obligation.

Nietzche's 'will to power' was, according to Tillich, 'a desig-
nation of the dynamic self-affirmation of life' and 'the drive of
everything living to realise itself with increasing intensity and
extensity, overcoming internal and external resistance' (Tillich,
1960: 36). Power, in this perspective, is the possibility of
overcoming non-being and is real only insofar as it is actualized
in and through the encounter with the Other. As therapists we
are required to overcome our own internal resistance to non-
being, our tendency to use the Other to bolster our sense of our
own being; instead we must strive to realize, acknowledge,
contain and restrain our power in the therapeutic interaction.

> The petty tyrannical doctor ... is better than the jovial
> healer who no longer even takes the trouble to dominate
> his patients. This cheerful, relaxed fellow has either
> repressed one pole of the archetype so severely that it can
> no longer be projected, or else he has never really been
> concerned with the basic problem of the physician and
> his choice of profession was merely superficial.
> (Güggenbühl-Craig, 1971, 1999: 88)

The therapist's task is to thwart the attempts of the client to
make her the source of all knowledge; she must encourage the
disruption of all answers, including those which reside in the
therapist. We must rather assist clients (should they so decide)
to realize and access their own will-to-power, to dismantle the
patterns of power relations which have hitherto dominated their
lives.

> Caring ... appears to be humble yet is anything but. To
> the contrary it stems from an arrogance, the arrogance of
> knowledge and power – or at least assumed knowledge.
> For the carer knows what is wrong with the other, knows
> what the other needs, better of course than she herself,
> and has the power to do something about it ... The
> therapist, despite denials, is the one who *knows* what is
> going on. After all she has read the books ... she has
> been *trained*, and ... is registered and has a certificate to
> prove it. (Gordon, 1999: 23)

We take heed of Gordon's sardonic warning. A 'radical respect
for persons' implies an alertness to our tendency to use others for
our own benefit, together with a willingness systematically to
address this tendency in our dealings with others. In the practice
of psychotherapy the temptation to proceed on the basis of an

assumption of our own 'goodness' makes it particularly difficult to avoid castigating the client when therapy fails to 'cure' rather than exploring our own actions, scrutinizing our conscious motivation to 'help'.

Similarly, in the field of education it is all too easy for the teacher to lack respect for the student. Any sense of complacency encourages an arrogance which constitutes a dangerous state of affairs for teacher or therapist; such a state of 'knowing' creates a closed system impermeable to the Other.

Entrée into this field promises a professional (if not a personal) life of discomfort, uncertainty, surprise and discovery. Thomas Szasz speaks of: 'the practice of dignified dialogue as therapy ...', and goes on: 'There are other things the psychotherapist must know and be, among which, in my opinion, the two most important are: making and keeping promises and personal integrity' (Szasz, 1992: 3). This applies equally to the undertaking of the teacher. A colleague speaks of 'walking the talk'; in other words attempting to embody the ethical principles of which we write, and which roll easily off the tongue when one is standing in front of students – not such a simple task when one attempts to 'stand side by side with the Other'.

Repairing the World

> ... Incomplete, becoming, the world
> was given to us to fix, to complete
> and we've almost worn it out ... (Piercy, 1998: 82)

Psychotherapy is only one small strand of possibility, one strategy that people might follow when in distress or when wishing to change something about themselves or their lives. Some of us have chosen this particular mode of involving ourselves with the world of persons; we believe it to be the best way for us to implement an intention to repair, and to 'give something back'. But what we're about is more than that – what we attempt is nothing less than social engineering, a (r)evolutionary activity, albeit on an individual scale. We would not undertake such an activity unless we believed that the influence of the encounter reaches beyond the consulting room, permeating this person's life outside, her social realm and the world beyond. What an outrageous belief; what an outrageous undertaking! But as we find ourselves drawn towards 'helping' others in this particular one-to-one fashion, we notice we have mixed motives for doing so, and so we must be careful how we go about this particular way of being together with these particular others.

> ... psychotherapy cannot be isolated from ordinary living – that is ordinary living in an unusual situation; it has a social context ... the simple aim of helping those in anguish by means of talking to them. (Lomas, 2001: 11)

H: I would go further. I do not see psychotherapy or the many alternative routes to contemplation, reflection, and exploration as a luxury, or simply for those in 'anguish'. I am bewildered at how we expect to be able to live our lives healthily without having the space to acknowledge our experience, to notice our sensations, to reflect upon our reactions, to think something through, to grieve, or simply be able to share ourselves in a safe, secure environment – to process. Psychotherapy may have appeared as a twentieth-century phenomenon, but setting time aside to 'be with oneself' – to contemplate, dates back to early civilization, and has a central role within every civilization. In Judaism you speak of *teshuvah* (returning) and again perhaps we are simply returning to ancient wisdom with our present-day vision. For the individual it takes strength and courage to be with myself, and wisdom to realize that there is little choice. Often the struggle for client and student alike (if not all of us throughout our lifetimes) is the recognition of the simple fact that perhaps my most important and demanding relationship is the one with myself.

> This above all – to thine own self be true,
> And it must follow, as the night the day,
> Thou canst not then be false to any man. (Shakespeare, *Hamlet*, Act 1, scene 3: lines 78–80)

Confidence in Humanity

'Ordinary living in an unusual situation' – what are the values that inform a praxis – a 'lived' psychotherapy – towards which this book is orientated? Once again, when standing in front of a class of trainees to what extent am I knowingly presenting myself as a model? And if so, a model of what? We consider that as teachers of psychotherapy we seek to embody a radical responsibility for the learner, as onerous and uncomfortable as this may be. We acknowledge that any such attempt can only ever achieve partial success. We must remain alert and questioning of the quality of our engagement in this context.

No psychotherapist could take up this occupation without a fundamental attitude of optimism about humanity, of confidence in the human capacity to change, to 'self-actualise', as Abraham Maslow put it. Equally, one could not teach psychotherapy without a conviction that students have a similar capacity to change, and to develop skills, attitudes and abilities which go beyond common expectation. But as it is more difficult to 'trust the client' who is stuck, or seemingly resistant to change, or presenting a challenge to one's capacity to bear confusion, so it is equally difficult to 'trust the student' to know the limits of her 'comfort zone', or to develop his own developmental rhythm, when these moments may seem to pose a threat to the teacher's sense of professional competence or come into conflict with a deeply entrenched and perhaps unexplored bias or prejudice.

Ethics and Professionalism

In my work as a psychotherapist, I am on my honour when I enter that private space with an Other. Honour and integrity are ethical precepts which should, and must be incorporated into any definition of 'professionalism'. And yet at the beginning of the 21st century the idea of 'profession' has become tarnished, seen as often setting disappointing standards for its members, while offering shelter to dubious characters – perpetuating a separatist view of existence dividing those who 'know' and those whose 'seek' that knowledge.

The 'profession' of psychotherapy stands at a critical juncture in its history. It can opt to stand alongside other 'professions', gaining status and recognition by those more 'established', or it can remain true to its radical, questioning nature attempting to warrant the title of 'honourable profession' – standing at the vanguard of 'not-knowing' with all the struggle and discomfort that that entails.

Responsibility

To become a psychotherapist is to shoulder a considerable degree of responsibility for the Other; in fact, I offer myself as a trustworthy recipient of the profoundest secrets and deepest fears of clients.

M: I'm interested in the consequences of what could be conceptualized as 'the discovery of the unconscious', the decentring of the human subject from him or herself. For me, the term 'unconscious' functions as a useful, if loose, expression that encapsulates

155

my lack of awareness, of understanding, of moment-to-moment insight into the workings of my mind/body. This decentring does not imply any dilution in my responsibility for my actions, and for the consequences, however unintended, of those actions. Precisely to the contrary, my awareness of how I am driven by motivations and impulses of which I am unaware only underlines how I must work at my responsibility, consistently subjecting to examination my mode of being and my actions in light of an interpersonal perspective.

Equally significant is the 'melancholy, long, withdrawing roar' (Arnold, 1972) of belief in a supernatural Creator who directs and controls the world and whom we can hold responsible for events in the world. The widespread loss of such a religious faith deprives us of a revelatory guide, a 'top-down' codification of how to conduct our lives. Our questioning rationality and a widespread awareness of the inner corruption inherent in all human institutions has encouraged the universalizing of the idea of human rights, and an associated common ethical code gradually permeating throughout the world. Thus we take responsibility away from a superior being into ourselves.

H: So much of our work is around the challenge of engaging with the unknown, grappling with the magic and mystery, which includes the inescapable tragedy of human existence.

This is the major development we see that goes alongside psychotherapy, the self-with-Other examination of the human subject. This learning unquestionably constitutes progress, learning more about what it means to be an agent with responsibility, with intention. And as we continue to pay attention to our responsibility for the Other within the specific sphere of therapy training, we rest in confidence, that whatever is 'taught', individuals will learn what they learn. We see an expanding sense of possibilities in being less defensive, more open to the Other. Hopefully this learning can be carried forward, rippling out into the world . . .

H: Yes, that is our hope. I think it is a critical time in terms of world history to be discussing ethics – there appears to be a striking absence of a consideration of ethics in much of the world; almost the absence of the awareness of the concept itself, which raises the question: 'To what code of relation between people are we operating?'.

M: Yet has it ever been otherwise? I believe the old 'religion-based' morality was never an integrated, owned, ethical awareness, but an externally imposed set of rules often more breached than observed. And yet MacMurray agreed with you, I think. He critiqued capitalism for 'canonising competition and self-interest and for making economic values primary and independent, instead of situating them within and subordinating them to the values of co-operation and community' (MacMurray, 935, 1992: 5).

H: And so we come full circle back to the idea of teaching and what it is we are teaching, and by virtue of being teachers, what it is that we embody. I find what you've said very thought-provoking. It reminds me of the idea of 'the letter of the law *v.* the substance', and the arguments I used to have with my father (the son of a *Talmud* scholar, and himself a lawyer). I think the same principle applies to any 'code'. It is not enough to follow the rules simply because they are the rules – in whatever context. In order to implicate myself in my actions I must examine and question my choices all the time. In order to embody an ethical stance it is essential to 'help' students develop skills of discernment, to become an internalized resource to call upon when they find themselves in the confines of the therapeutic setting.

> Psychotherapy must remain an obstinate attempt of two people to recover the wholeness of being human through the relationship between them. (Laing, 1967: 45)

H: Psychotherapy training must encompass a way of grappling with ethical questions as well as facilitating students' thinking through the ethical dimensions of any given situation. I would agree that psychotherapy and the training to become a therapist can play a positive part in our relations with each other, beyond the confines of the consulting room, and beyond the learning environment. I too am very hopeful about this; am often in awe of what I see take place, of what I have the privilege of taking part in. Our sense of psychotherapy as a 'radical enterprise' is precisely this notion of psychotherapy at its best, as profound illustration of the potentiality of what can take place between people.

H: It concerns me that often as teachers we do not 'walk the talk'. It concerns me that often therapeutic ideals get left at the classroom door, and our human-to-human engagement falls short. Courtesy, kindness, consideration, the recognition of the Other often get lost in the busy-ness of the day, or overshadowed by the conflicting concern for a maintenance of professional boundaries. In Buberian terms maintaining an I–Thou stance demands a constant openness. When the person becomes 'a student' I have turned away, become remote, and immunized.

The therapeutic process often entails a 'slowing down' in order to listen to oneself, and the other, in order to be able to hear. To attempt to stay in that place of listening, hearing, noticing can be very frightening and therefore knowingly, or unknowingly, is often avoided. As teachers we hope to have the courage and strength to attempt to model just that, bearing in mind our dual responsibility: the personal (and therefore professional) development of the trainee and the safety and well-being of their 'clients to be'. We are gatekeepers, whose task is to 'let through' those who can demonstrate their competence, and to 'shut out' those who may conceivably constitute a danger to prospective clients – the judgement of Solomon, in effect, since all of us will have miserably failed clients.

Self-deception and Truthfulness

> If we cannot live with our need to renew agreements we have made, we break the only promise we really owe each other – to be truthful. This means finding both the courage to be truthful with ourselves and a way to live with how our actions affect others, even when there is no ill intent and no one to blame. (Oriah Mountain Dreamer, 1999: 62)

> The only 'trueness' in terms of actual psychic reality is found in emotion, not in thinking, which at best denies or rationalises truth, and not necessarily in action unless it follows from feeling and is in harmony with it. (Rank, 1936: 40)

Psychotherapy, along with other activities encompassed in what are described as the 'caring professions', is often characterized as an altruistic activity. People who apply to train in psychotherapy very often describe their motivation as a desire to 'help' others. While respecting such intent, a watchfulness is necessary, as the desire to help may harbour and disguise more self-serving motives, which require some system, whether internal or external, of monitoring, of checks and balances, lest they act to the detriment of those whom we wish to help.

Evolutionary biologists have hypothesized that 'human beings have a natural, evolved tendency towards breaking the rules of society' (Smith, 1999: 8, 9). Such rule-breaking is a form of cheating, they claim: rule-breakers do not wish to be found out, since most forms of cheating are inevitably subject to penalties of one kind or another. Language helps us cheat, because it enables us to misrepresent our actions – to lie. The complex nature of human social interaction is built and maintained on the basis of the 'little white lie'. To protect ourselves, and to assist in our agenda of deception, the complex nature of the human brain/mind allows us to deceive ourselves, the better to deceive others. What better insurance could there be against giving the show away than remaining unaware of one's own dishonesty?

And what are the ethical implications of our determined unawareness of our complex motivations in our interactions with others? Freud commended us, 'Be as moral as you can honestly be and do not strive for an ethical perfection for which you are not destined' (Hale, 1971: 122).

So face it: we all deny, exaggerate, dramatize, pretend, lie, deceive, both ourselves and others. Frank points out how, paradoxically, such 'rationalizations' are the necessary illusions that both cover up and articulate truth. Arguably, while 'Freudian slips' glaringly, and dreams more subtly, reveal our deception when some 'correction' becomes necessary, '[t]o be able to live one needs illusion ...' (Rank, 1936: 42).

We would maintain that the agenda of truthfulness must be fundamental to an ethical psychotherapy, and that, if this includes the willingness to acknowledge our responsibility for the roots and implications of our own actions, we will be better equipped to enact our radical responsibility for the Other.

It takes courage to undertake the self-examination, the openness, and the self-acceptance that Freud saw as a necessary and primary ethical act (Wallwork, 1991: 289). In addition, Richard Holloway (1999) points to the principle of consent (we would say informed consent): consensual agreement between our own reason and emotion, and between ourselves and the Other with whom we are in relation. Such a principle, as an extension of the truthfulness we propose as fundamental, should assist us in our efforts to counter the tendency towards the inevitable power imbalance in the therapeutic relationship.

Disclosure and Self-examination

> But in a legitimate effort to claim authority in our lives, we forget that there is a reality beyond our limited perception – if not objective, at the least, intersubjective. If I get up tomorrow and see two suns shining in the sky, the first thing I will do is ask someone else what they see. ... We can be and sometimes are wrong. Knowing this, we can create community where we can check to see if our perceptions have any intersubjective truth. Of course, ultimately, we must decide which perceptions we will grant validity. But to insist that 'my truth' and 'your truth' have no meeting place, that I do not need to consider other perspectives – to be unable to imagine that I may be wrong about what I think or see or feel at any given time – is to invite narcissistic mayhem. (Oriah Mountain Dreamer, 1999: 75)

What is misleadingly known as 'supervision' in some ways encompasses the function of monitoring practice. If this aspect is too strongly emphasized it will undermine the relationship between supervisor and supervisee, often leading to a self-protective stance which does not encourage disclosure and self-with-other examination – a learning process beneficial to practice for therapist and client – so that problem areas can be tackled and hopefully surmounted, not condoned, but not condemned either. If we can let go of the 'Thou shalt not' aspect, in favour of a consideration of how 'one shalt be with an other', and of what is honourable in the given circumstances, while at the same time honouring one's own principles; then something strong and valuable can emerge.

H: Confidentiality, respect for the autonomy of the other person – elements we see as fundamental – are at risk of being overshadowed by an alien 'policing' role. The policing of oneself is an ethical imperative for teacher, learner and practitioner.

M: Within the structures of the profession one can see the place of supervision as an extension of one's own watchfulness towards practice, behaviour, etc. In a sense I give myself over, feeling safe enough to expose and consider what has taken place, how I have been with an Other.

> We have all been the betrayer and the betrayed. If we cannot acknowledge this, we will find ourselves harsh and unforgiving, unable to grieve for the times we have betrayed ourselves ... The real damage of betrayal is in the lies we tell one another and ourselves, the lies that cause us to lose faith in our ability to recognize and act on the truth. (Oriah Mountain Dreamer, 1999: 64)

Therapy is such an intensely personal affair that it is easy for an outsider, using his own personal equation, to misunderstand what is going on. Supervision, therefore, does not always provide the definitive answer. Güggenbühl-Craig's recommended solution (1999) is friendship, a relationship symmetrical in love with partner, friends, family, who dare to lovingly confront, challenge, ridicule and support me; intensive interpersonal relationships through which I am accompanied as I continue in my journey towards a 'good death'.

The Tower of Babel

An ethical stance towards my engagement with an Other, as demonstrated in the therapeutic context, demands that I recognize my client as Other, that I abandon a great many certainties, along with preconceptions and assumptions about my relations with others, and be willing to attempt to develop an attitude or position of openness towards the Other in all her strangeness which avoids reducing her to what is already known to me, and allows for her 'different' perception of me in return.

'Difference' is a theme which follows each of us through life – my difference from you; your difference from me; my difference from myself at another time remembered, or anticipated. Some notice difference, others are blind to it. Our discomfort with the notion of change, be it within ourselves, someone close to us, or our circumstances is all about difference – about the unknown, the unfamiliar.

Difference is a paradoxical concept. It could more accurately be presented as 'difference-sameness'. It is as if there is an invisible continuum from one to the other; up to a certain point someone/something is recognizable, familiar, enough like me that I remain comfortable – beyond a certain point, the degree of 'difference' takes me into an unfamiliar realm, challenges me, my values, beliefs.

My respect for the Other leads me to a sense of wonder, and curiosity, when I attempt to come close to another's experience.

I relinquish the inclination to take what I hear and situate it in categories familiar to me. I struggle to remain with our 'in-the-moment' engagement and not to resort to any of the myriad of techniques which will make the process more comfortable for me, while diminishing my client.

M: There is something about difference: denial of difference can become identification, or over-identification. The polarity sameness/difference may well be a familiar arena of personal and interpersonal struggle for others, as it is for me; so I wanted to say, in balance, that one of the things I glory in is the difference, when the other is just so different, that I feel enormously challenged – the meeting is stimulating and intense.

H: Pronounced difference also has a cleanness, a clarity about it; in effect: 'This is either going to be an adventure or a disaster ...'

M: But also it is a hard surface, a frontier, being there in unexplored territory.

In a sense, how I am as a practitioner or teacher when confronted with difference in all its overt and subtle guises is a benchmark of the fulfilment of my ethical undertaking. My encounter with difference unleashes a multitude of sensations, challenges my attitudes, my values, my so-called knowledge base, causes confusion, disruption, hostility and fear – takes me, often involuntarily, beyond myself into unfamiliar territory. This is the business of being-with an Other – the 'business' for which I train, discipline and galvanize myself.

7
After Theory

We approached the task of writing this book without quite knowing where or how we would end up.

All the way through we have been in dialogue with each other and with 'the others': others who have written down their thoughts, distilling their experience and their hard-won wisdom; others with whom we work – clients, students and colleagues. From all of these we have learnt and will continue to learn; some will also learn with us.

The dialogue between us has not been restricted to teaching/learning psychotherapy – if it were so it would not be dialogue. We came together to undertake the book, but also out of a recognition of some sameness and some difference between us, and we have been exploring this terrain through the work. We have approached the task out of a shared sense of responsibility and a trust in each other which is founded on our sense of an identity of interest. Very often what is common to us matters less than what differentiates us, and that difference can be threatening to acknowledge and articulate. Yet in this relationship we also find the kind of meaning that gives life to our joint undertaking.

The process is also the content. The form of this dialogue embodies, however imperfectly, some aspects of teaching/learning psychotherapy.

What we have been proposing, and discussing, throughout the book is a model of learning which emphasizes the 'personal' – the interpersonal, the relational, the mode of the individual's being-together-with-others – over the intellectual. Considerable research (e.g. Bergin and Garfield, 1994; Aveline and Shapiro, 1995; Roth and Fonagy, 1996) supports the overwhelming significance of the therapeutic relationship itself as the 'healing' factor in psychotherapy and counselling; theories and models seem largely irrelevant:

> ... while it is legitimate to conclude that we may not know just why it is likely that psychotherapeutic input will have beneficial consequences, or what the critical factors are that may increase their prospect, it would be false to conclude that psychotherapy does not 'work'. It does; and it does so most of the time. It is the 'how and what' of it that continues to befuddle both practitioners and researchers. (Spinelli, 2001: 6)

Nonetheless, any teaching programme needs a syllabus. As teachers we 'select' what students will be presented with, based on what we consider important for them to learn; we make decisions, based on our own predilections and experience, in regard to the ordering and style of presentation. We believe we understand something of the process of development, which is a 'learning', or 'training'; we articulate a set of criteria in order to judge whether that developmental process has been effective.

The Value of Theory

> We need a language adequate to the times we inhabit ...
> we need words to keep us human ... Our needs are made

166

of words; they come to us in speech, and they can die for lack of expression ... Without the light of language, we risk becoming strangers to our better selves. (Ignatieff, 1984: 142)

Clearly, theory has its uses.

Theory introduces a valuable third party into the dyadic teacher/learner situation in psychotherapy training, a reference point, a third voice into the dialogue. Initially, it is useful to have the wherewithall to think, an already existing language through which we may enter into the particular conversation that is the ground of teaching/learning. Theory – the text, the articulation of the experience of an absent Other – is a component in the chemistry of individual development, and in the necessary development of a new language. It is important to have learners develop the means to think; at times to present a language for their learning, but they must be free to choose or to develop that language for themselves ...

We are always selecting, and even working with the text itself: we will tend to put it in a different way, in our own words, which inevitably presents our 'take' on the author's work. Like it or not, I am a filter through which learners will come to the text. In selecting what I find important or significant and presenting it to students, I omit another idea or opinion, with which I may be having some difficulty. There is a danger that I avoid the responsibility of saying what I feel about this other aspect. It is all too easy to take a position of owning material that is the outcome of someone else's creative process. It may be 'dead' text until I take it unto myself and make it something alive through me. But then the danger is that this forecloses the range of possibility for the text to enter into dialogue with another.

We have talked about embodying: I present the material, and I also present myself in relation to the text; I allow myself to be

167

situated, contextualized within the moment and by the text. In these moments, too, arises the question of the nature and quality of my relation to the text that I am presenting. If I am teaching an area with which I'm unfamiliar or to which I do not subscribe, I may find myself presented with an ethical dilemma: how to be fair to the material, fair to myself, while attempting to maintain an open, collaborative rapport with my students. My relationship with the material becomes part of my relationship with the learner ...

There is a value in engaging with the ideas, as we have done in this book – there are so many really powerful and interesting ideas that have been set forth by the 'ancients' – the wise ones. 'There is no theory that is not a fragment, carefully prepared, of some autobiography' (Valéry, 1977: 142); and the most interesting and relevant 'theories' are those born out of profound personal learning: 'In our sleep, pain which cannot forget falls drop by drop upon the heart until, in our own despair, against our will, comes wisdom through the awful grace of God' (Yusuf, 2002).

Yet we recognize that the process of conceptualizing itself is a retreat from our own lived experience. Ultimately we each have to learn for ourselves, to check the ideas of others against our own experience and value systems, which is why the wisdom of the Other so often falls on deaf ears. So we must be clear that teaching as opposed to initiating or indoctrinating is about offering many alternative ways of understanding what it means to be human. We therefore have to work hard at how we address theory – the ideas and hypotheses of others – and to clarify what it is we hope to achieve through the process of engagement with theory. However, no matter to what extent we might try to mitigate it, the intellectual process does tend to get siphoned off into a separate compartment. This says something not just about therapy, but about learning and studying in general, whether and how it's possible to learn in a more holistic way ...

168

In fact, there are many ways of coming at the 'it' of this learning (see Chapter 2), but experiential work – group-work, clinical supervision, practical sessions – allows for a particular sort of 'lived' learning – providing the opportunity for theoretical ideas to be grounded in whatever the experience may be. In the experiential aspect of learning/teaching each participant is asked to be part of the process, the setting allowing much more for this spirit of co-operation, or for the competitiveness, or whatever is available for the particular person at that time. And here there's a more immediate relation between teacher and learner; there is a shared experience into which the theory is integrated.

Each of us has her own unique, constantly fluctuating, repertoire of ways of being, and ways of being with another. However when we undertake to speak about 'being-with' with students of psychotherapy, there is no doubt that we have a very particular, if also highly elusive, notion in mind. Once again I attempt to embody the words; I seek to bring myself as fully as possible into my current situation, being alert to the environment around me, as well as the broader historical context, my own values, reactions and sensations, the fluctuations of atmosphere, etc., but perhaps most importantly having a willingness to go out from my own experience towards another's.

> After all, what is happening? Two people meet in a room and talk – or not. It is, Bion once remarked, absurdly simple, and yet 'so simple it's hard to believe how hard it is'. Too often the theories just prevent us seeing what is before us, this simple fact in all its complexity. (Gordon, 1999: 37)

Psychotherapy involves heart and soul and intellect – all my senses poised to notice, to engage, to care, to challenge – to meet another human being, to offer the potential for connection, the willingness to receive the client's story and the style of their being – to volunteer as witness, sounding-board, shoulder, advocate, willing partner in a process of reconsideration, reflection, struggle, argument, anger, disappointment, tedium, healing, warmth, love, joy, humour, satisfaction, growth, reconciliation – the list is endless, as is the potential for relation.

We speak of 'attitudes' and 'ways of being' rather than skills and competencies; we emphasize our own particular, very personal 'ways of being' towards each other, seeking to attempt to remain open to such challenges as 'uncertainty, insecurity, and receptiveness towards the unforeseen possibilities of a human (and humane) engagement with another ... The abdication of the security that comes with assumptions such as "doing it right" or directing change, or of "the expert's superiority of knowledge and status"' (Spinelli, 2001: 14) is, we believe, the 'stuff' of the therapeutic attitude.

It comes full circle, to what we embody as teachers, for which we have to take full responsibility. While we may not wish to advocate a 'mentor' approach, we nevertheless take on that role, and propose ourselves as 'embodied theories' (Spinelli and Marshall, 2001), aware that we will embody and show more, and less, than we intend – that we will never fully succeed, but that the demonstration of our ongoing struggle is a modelling in itself.

After Theory

> The profession of psychotherapy is now resting on a hundred years of intensive and sincere effort to glean complex and valuable insights into the nature of the psyche, but it is important to recognize that theory can only facilitate our ways of understanding and feeling more for the client. (Pearmain, 2001: 128)

Psychotherapy, like most other fields, suffers from competition for power and rival claims to 'the truth'. The plethora of theories within the field, akin to political ideologies or religious belief systems, all attempt to unravel and master – some would say 'colonize' – the mystery of what it is to be human. Often the function of our psychotherapeutic allegiances is to divide, separate and alienate in a way similar to other 'belief' allegiances. It is truly a 'Tower of Babel' situation, each orientation a closed system complete with intricate schemata and language to guard against intrusion, facilitating and perpetuating the gulf between would-be colleagues.

But as we said at the outset, psychotherapy is at an exciting point in its history, a time when the divisions between some theoretical positions (within some circles) are dissolving; a time when a psychoanalyst may speak of the 'intersubjective', and an 'integrative stance' is now regarded with respect – a time when an existential-phenomenological psychotherapist and a communicative psychotherapist can collaborate!

Many voices now acknowledge that the value of our work is ultimately its endeavour to facilitate more successful human contact at all levels of social engagement. We psychotherapists can now acknowledge that theory provides us with useful anchors, symbols and metaphors with which to conceptualize, categorize and ground our lived experience of being human and of being-in-relation. It provides us with a multitude of possibilities while we continue to ponder the 'the big questions'. It provides us with a language to speak of our experience and that of an Other, but not more. We must avoid the 'compulsion to make sense' (Kurtz, cited in Gordon, 1999: 90, 91).

> To experience the patient's words openly, without passing them through a pre-formed cognitive screen, can occasion great anxiety. The defences erected against this anxiety

171

have found institutional expression in analytic theory and practice. In so doing, they are instances of a greater fear of unknowing that pervades the Western mind. The compulsion to make sense will only hold attunement back, leaving the patient misunderstood, isolated and unloved.
(Kurtz, cited in Gordon, 1999: 90–91)

The danger of theory is that it functions to distance learner from being-with learning, and therapist from being-with client. Theory acts in the learning context as a shield against opening oneself up to the personal meeting with learning, or with the Other. In therapy theory erects an interpersonal barrier within the therapeutic dyad, protecting the practitioner from the danger inherent in being close to, or part of, the experience of an other. Theory situates the client as an 'It', and thus stands in the way of 'meeting' and of the co-creation of new, shared meaning.

After Therapy

If theory is limited in its usefulness, its value, then so is therapy.

Doing therapy, becoming a practitioner, should always remain a questionable endeavour – one means, among many, to whatever may constitute 'personal development' for clients, through the experience of dialogue. The practice of psychotherapy may become an addiction, a form of spurious intimacy, a reparative activity that has its roots in an avoidance of 'real' living, or it may represent a manageable mode of 'repairing the world', beginning with Thou. Alternatively, psychotherapy may represent a way to allow me to feel 'strong' and 'good' in ways which are unavailable to me elsewhere.

As long as I recognize that my motivation may include none and/or all of the above, and as long as I can be open to learning from the Other, I may be helpful in my limited aims, towards being, and remaining, together with the Other with whom I am engaged in a particular conversation.

If that sounds unambitious, be reminded of the *very* ambitious overall project: we remain firmly convinced that psychotherapy, with its *sequelae*, takes its place alongside other (r)evolutionary endeavours playing a part in changing the world!

> Everything just happens ... and of course all this is as true of ourselves, our ideas, our words, our values, our thoughts and fears, as it is of the so-called external world. Notice that philosophically there is no difference between our world and the world, for such intelligibility and order as the world has it gets through us, in our seeing of it. In us the empty flux of be-ing gets coded into signs, because we see everything in terms of words, and numbers, and thereby make it all into a brightly lit, consciously seen and processed world of our own. Only through us does the world become world. (Cupitt, 2002: 25–6)

In the World

> ... human social relations as we normally find them are sadly distorted. The everyday being-with others ... does not flow from whole selves. The way in which people are normally together does not deserve the name of community. What we find is a distorting and distorted relationship ... (Macquarrie, 1972: 118)

Psychotherapy and psychotherapy training present a direct challenge to the individual to come out of the crowd and take upon herself the burden and the responsibility of being, of being-for-herself, of being-in-the-world, and of the choices that such a situation presents to each of us.

Some of what we have said may seem to be impossibly utopian: a vision of a microcosm of society in which we dream of overcoming the human tragedy of alienation between persons. The current status of 'lay' psychotherapy as a marginalized discipline is both an opportunity and a threat. It is an opportunity in that it remains a 'secret voice' – a still, small, reflective voice providing a tiny murmur of commentary on our actions, our behaviour as humans in the world. It is a threat insofar as its particular contribution to this universal conversation may be obscured by more influential groups claiming authority to speak on psychotherapy's behalf, who privilege a less personal and interpersonal, more 'medical' perspective. One of the dangers we have highlighted of the current project of 'professionalizing' psychotherapy is of a ceding of authority to an outdated 'scientism' that (if we allow it) may, in defining the discipline as a 'profession allied to medicine', confine and reduce its creative propensities.

Yet in this collaboration we feel we have created a safe space for ourselves, wherein we feel free to say what we think, to make fools of ourselves, and to say 'I don't like that.' We would hope that a similar freedom is created within the teaching/learning setting, and we suggest it is possible to take that attitude out into the wider social context.

H: I believe that what goes on inside the consulting room should not be that different from what goes on outside of it. Therapy does indeed require a disciplined approach which includes the expectation of a less explicit reciprocity than may be hoped for, or than may be possible, in the world of 'ordinary' relationships; but I think it is sad that we therapists are often seen to reserve 'the best of ourselves' for our clients. We work with a repertoire of capacities common to us all, and our intention in the training situation is to assist learners to hone and develop those capacities further, to the extent that they engage with an Other more knowingly while 'working'. But what does it mean to be 'off duty'? As we said earlier, 'a dialogic stance is not something you don' – it is something you strive to embody in your everyday encounters with existence. What we teach/learn in this field – how to be-with an Other – shouldn't be isolated, and siphoned off into the rarified atmosphere of the consulting room, but we hope will extend into how we express our humanity in all facets of our lives. The learning must branch out in both directions – otherwise what are we learning?

M: That may be an area of divergence between us because of my sense that the 'therapeutic attitude' is, to a degree, an 'unnatural' stance. In the context of psychotherapy we have (we hope) developed the capacity to notice when we become defensive and become more able to acknowledge and 'work through' our defensiveness in certain ways. But we are programmed or hard-wired for self-interest, survival and self-protection, which includes deception and self-deception, and we'd be fools to imagine we can get around that. Hopefully we have learnt that we can choose to adopt other modes of being, ways of more fully 'being-for-the-Other', that what I am proposing as an unnatural stance can become more 'natural'. We must ensure that our revolutionary aims remain limited, after all, and that we situate them within an achievable, evolutionary time-frame!

H: I see things the other way around. What I see is more the struggle to regain ourselves – our 'natural' attunement to existence, which we have gone so far away from. We forget we are part of nature, but we see it in children. They demonstrate an openness, a knowing, and an acute awareness of the physical and emotional world around them. Children are less fearful than adults – generally, they learn fear from adults. Self-interest, the fight for survival and self-protection are aspects of us that develop out of fear, and it is very sad when we allow ourselves to be defined and limited by them.

We are given the opportunity of life. That is a responsibility. Given the world we live in, I feel my task is always to be striving – striving to be more present to myself and others – aware of the world and those around me, less guarded, less self-protective. The Hasidic, Jewish tradition speaks of the 'sanctification of the everyday', which refers to the capacity to notice and to be respectful of the detail of life, to see oneself in and of it. Similarly, Buddhists talk of the practice of 'mindfulness'. That is our daily work and it is never-ending.

M: This may be a difference in our attitudes, that you hold to a more positive view of how we may be as persons in the world, while I represent a 'darker' view. I am more likely to recognize the context of anxiety and even terror which fuels our many ways of being defended and defensive . . .

H: Our difference seems to centre on the role of 'fear'. Fear is at the centre of the therapeutic project, whether it shows itself as fear of intimacy, of death, or even of succeeding – of 'shining' (Mandela, 1994) – precisely of coming out of the crowd. As I see it, fear is a key part of our life project – the challenge to face our fears, no matter in what guise they show themselves.

Having said that, we both want to remake the world; we want to be part of the same overall project, but we may have different perspectives on what it means to be human, and different expectations about the desired outcome of our work of being-with.

M: In view of all this, what is training for? Some people have a natural aptitude for listening in this particular way, yet there is also a discipline involved in this that must be learnt, a curriculum of 'unlearning', in order to be able to be 'neutral', or to be governed by the principle of 'concern for the other'. It may be more easily understood if it were to be described as a spiritual discipline, yet that description, for many, would militate against a 'professional' approach. I don't see it that way; yet I wouldn't want to deny an aspect of 'vocation' in my motivation.

H: Gordon's critique (1999) is that we seek to 'professionalize' qualities of being human: that we claim not only to know best about what's wrong with you, but also that we know how to talk to you better than somebody else. That's how we make our living – we buy into that – yet it's a highly questionable stance to take.

So we come back to how we as teachers take responsibility for embodying, for carrying through into behaviour, the values and modes of being that we 'teach'. Having left one profession, I felt I was moving from one way of responding to people to another, from concrete to abstract, a way that more adequately fulfilled my need to 'meet' others, entailed less doing and more being; I believe that therapy could lead the way in another direction instead of attempting to join the game.

M: And this is part of our agenda in this discussion: what next? What lies after theory, after training, after psychotherapy?

What we've described as a 'frame' – of teaching/learning, of being-in-the-world – tends to dissolve and change as we speak, so that we are continually making and remaking the frame. The world of human society in all its dimensions is in a state of 'dynamic disequilibrium'; we reach for and are nostalgic for the 'certainties' we were fed as children. So we look to someone else to take responsibility; we exist in a culture which looks for someone to blame; we demand compensation or retribution

177

for human fallibility as it affects us. We look for easy, reductionist solutions to the dilemmas of human existence. There's a problem – let's say of 'madness' (psychosis, 'schizophrenia') – the 'solution' is perceived to lie in improved pharmacology and in legislation. We collude in the delusion that if we put right this little bit here, that little bit there, we have no need to look more deeply within ourselves.

H: As things change in the way human society understands itself, the way it conducts itself, we need to dig our heels in and say that we prefer 'being' to knowing, or to doing. We would therefore favour the creation of new structures, so that, rather than trying to fit the person into a pre-existing structure, we should seek to create structures that work for human beings. Freud began this project, and arguably got side-tracked ...

M: His new paradigm was subversive, but arguably not subversive enough ...

Subversion

A key part of the learning we have described for both teachers and learners is the difficult task of stepping into the shoes of the Other, not just another of my ilk, but a being who is wholly alien, who holds values which I reject with my whole being. Do not underestimate how subversive this may be: the ultimate task in this would be to contain and manage my feelings, my revulsion, my horror, my anger, or my terror, in order to stay with *this* Other here and now. In this way both parties must struggle to stay in the room, each of us grappling with the fear that a glimpse into the world of the Other will threaten my equilibrium within my given value-system. This may apply to the experience of teaching, as to that of therapy.

It seems impossible that the competing claims of myself and this Other could ever be satisfactorily reconciled. Power remains deaf to the claim of the Other to be heard. Yet, out of our learning and our experience in the particular context we have been discussing, we would insist, rather, that it is possible to seek to engage with this Other, to see his face, to meet his eyes, to hear who he is and to imagine who and what he loves, in a way which may be seen as analogous to the 'dialogic attitude' we have been proposing. By going out to the Other in this fashion, we not only seek to create the possibility of true dialogue, but recognize that we may hear some unpalatable 'feedback', that we may 'see ourselves as others see us' (Burns, 1993: 86). This is what we must learn to bear.

We must be clear about the cost: I am required to come out from behind my comfortable position of 'knowing' I am right; I become 'unaccommodated man ... a poor, bare, forked animal as thou art' (Shakespeare, *King Lear*, Act 3, scene 4: lines 105–6). The Other then has an equal claim to be right. Such a claim may demand action from me, whether that be through the word of witness inside the consulting room or through more substantive action as a teacher and 'out there' in the world.

Again, however, we see the importance of having an awareness of what it is that has to be set on one side, in order to be-with the Other. In order to deal with the otherness of the Other, I need to call upon my own experience of being a stranger, of having left 'home', of being homeless, or of having been marginalized.

H: So far as my 'homelessness' is an integral part of my history, I want to know about it, even if such knowledge complicates things for me.

M: It complicates things, but if you can explore it, you can then explore the discomfort.

H: That's true – without knowledge I can't name what's bothering me.

If there is, then, a lesson in all of this, it relates to a developing ability in the learning therapist (which includes all of us, no matter how old, or how experienced) to tolerate 'not-knowing', to be able to live with uncertainty, to maintain an inquisitiveness into how others have sought to manage their dilemmas, while attempting to manage our own daily challenges of being in relation with the Other/s.

Postscript

H: You were talking about Buber and MacMurray – the idea of the poet and metaphysicist – and about our different styles. In some ways I think our collaboration has been one of the best things about the book. I still marvel at our rapport, while finding it disheartening that it seems to be such a rare thing. I am not a saint: I can be very bossy, controlling, competitive, I'm not very trusting of the Other. Of course, I'm exaggerating a little, but those elements are there, so … I'm proud of myself, I'm proud of us, and excited, and heartened by what we've achieved. I grappled with so many of my undermining, isolating tendencies. It was very uncomfortable at times, but ultimately so satisfying. It has truly been a profound learning.

One of the things we share is a sense of ourselves as part of the world, and there's something for me about feeling like we have got some sort of place, in a fairly abstract way, something about not wanting to disrupt the equilibrium, not needing to colonize. Having a long-standing sense as individuals of being part of the world, and implicated in it, leads to us feeling we are part of the same thing – even though we do have very different histories, etc., and we seem, in our interaction, to be able to bridge that somehow …

181

M: I think so ... I've been surprised, and proud, as you say, because there has been so much enjoyment. There have been numerous difficulties, but we have been able to ride that ... There's something about inhabiting a collaborative landscape where we are reading the environment and the Other, and we are kind of navigating it, I suppose. The spiritual dimension in both of us has been stimulated.

H: I enjoy the use of the words magic, and mystery; I accept that I'm not about to receive 'the answers', but I feel that I am entitled, am obligated in fact, to play a part, nonetheless. You and I both come from strong theological or spiritual backgrounds and we have both gone our individual, independent ways ... The essence for me is always about a questioning attitude as I face the world . .. secretly, I remain ever hopeful.

M: My hope is for an always-active 'restored imagination', an aesthetic awareness which allows me to see the Other, to stand in the shoes of the Other ...

Bibliography

Albom, M. (1997), *Tuesdays with Morrie*. New York: Doubleday.

Arlow, J. (1993), 'Discussion of "The mind of the analyst"'. *International Journal of Psycho-Analysis*, 74, pp. 147–55.

Arnold, M. (1972), 'Dover Beach'. In *New Oxford Book of English Verse*. Oxford: Oxford University Press.

Aveline, M. and Shapiro, D. A. (1995), *Research Foundations for Psychotherapy Practice*. Chichester: Wiley.

Baranger, M. and Baranger, W. (1990), 'Insight in the Analytic Situation'. In Langs, R. (ed.), *Classics in Psychoanalytic Technique*. New York: Jason Aronson.

Bateson, G. (1958), *Naven* (2nd ed.). Stanford, CA: Stanford University Press.

Bateson, G. (2000), *Steps to an Ecology of Mind*. Chicago: University of Chicago Press.

Bauman, Z. (1993), *Postmodern Ethics*. Oxford: Blackwell.

Bergin, A. E. and Garfield, S. L. (1994), *Handbook of Psychotherapy and Behaviour Change* (4th ed.). Chichester: Wiley.

Bible, The (1971), London: Wm Collins Sons and Co.

Binswanger, L. (1963), *Being-in-the-World* (trans. Jacob Needleman). UK: Condor.

Bion, W. R. (1962), *Learning from Experience*. London: Heinemann.

Bleger, J. (1990), 'Psychoanalysis of the Psychoanalytic Frame'. In Langs, R. (ed.), *Classics in Psychoanalytic Technique*. New York: Jason Aronson.

Bollas, C. (1987), *The Shadow of the Object: Psychoanalysis of the Unthought Known*. New York: Columbia University Press.

Boss, M. (1979), *Existential Foundations of Medicine and Psychology*. London: Jacob Aronson, Inc.

Buber, M. (1958), *I And Thou* (trans. Ronald Gregor Smith). Edinburgh: T. and T. Clark.

Buber, M. (1947, 2002), *Between Man and Man*. London: Routledge.

Buber, M. (1965), *Between Man and Man*. New York: Macmillan.

Buber, M. (1988), *The Knowledge of Man* (edited, and with an introductory essay by M. Friedman, trans. R. G. Smith; introduction by A. Udoff). Atlantic Highlands, New Jersey: Humanities Press International Inc.

Burns, R. (1993), *Selected Poems*. London: Penguin.

Campart, M. (1996), 'Matching Modes of Teaching with Modes of Learning: a Review of Donald Meltzer's ideas'. In *Methods of Art as Paths to Knowledge* (eds R. Berg and M. Campart) Sweden: Lund University Publications.

Capra, F. (1997), *The Web of Life*. London: Flamingo.

Coltart, N. (1992), *Slouching Towards Bethlehem*. London: Free Association Books.

Critchley, S. (1992), *The Ethics of Deconstruction: Derrida and Levinas*. Oxford: Blackwell.

Cupitt, D. (2001), *Emptiness and Brightness*. Santa Rosa, California: Palbridge Press.

Figlio, K. (1993), 'The Field of Psychotherapy: Conceptual and Ethical Definitions'. *British Journal of Psychotherapy*, vol. 9 (3), pp. 324–35.

Figlio, K. (2002), Registration and Ethics in Psychotherapy. http://human-nature.com/free-associations/figlioreg.html.

Freire, P. (1972), *Pedagogy of the Oppressed*. London: Penguin.

Fromm, E. (1960), *Fear of Freedom*. London: Routledge.

Fromm, E. (1975), *The Art of Loving*. London: Penguin.

Frosh, S. (1999), *The Politics of Psychoanalysis* (2nd ed.). London: Macmillan Press.

Gans, S. and Redler, L. (2001), *Just Listening: Ethics and Therapy*. New York, Xlibris Corporation.

Gardner, F. (1995), 'Being in the Know: Thoughts on Training, Prestige and Knowledge'. *British Journal of Psychotherapy*, vol. 11 (3), 427–35.

Goldenberg, H. (1997), 'Stranger in a Strange Land', unpublished paper, Advanced Diploma in Existential Psychotherapy, SPC, Regents College: London.

Goldenberg, H. and Isaacson, Z. (1996), 'Between Persons: The Narrow Ridge Where I and Thou Meet', *Journal of the Society of Existential Analysis*, vol. 7, no. 2, 118–30.

Gordon P. (1999), *Face to Face: Therapy As Ethics*. London: Constable.

Grayling, A. C. (2002), *The Last Word on ... Might*. London: *Guardian*, 11 May 2002.

Grotstein, J. S. and Rinsley, D. B. (1994), *Fairbairn and the Origins of Object Relations*. London: Free Association Books.

Güggenbühl-Craig, A. (1999), *Power in the Helping Professions*. Putnam, CT: Spring Publications.

Hale, N. G. (ed.) (1971), *James Jackson Putnam and Psychoanalysis: Letters between Putnam and Sigmund Freud, Ernest Jones, Sandor Ferenczi, and Merton Prince, 1877–1917*. Cambridge, MA: Harvard University Press.

Heidegger, M. (1962), *Being and Time* (trans. John Macquarrie and Edward Robinson). Oxford: Blackwell.

Heidegger, M. (1977), *Martin Heidegger: Basic Writings*. (ed. D. Krell) San Francisco: Harper.

Hillel (1968), as in *Pirke Avot: The Sayings of the Fathers*, ed. B. Scharfstein. New York: Ktav Publishing House, Inc.

Holloway, R. (1999), *Godless Morality*. Edinburgh: Canongate.

House, R. (2001), 'The Statutory Regulation of Psychotherapy: Still Time to Think Again ...'. *The Psychotherapist*, issue 17.

Ignatieff, M. (1984), *The Needs of Strangers*. London: Hogarth Press.

Illich, I. (1997), *Disabling Professions*. London: Boyars.

Kennedy, R. (1998), *The Elusive Human Subject*. London: Free Association Books.

Kernberg, O. (1986), 'Institutional Problems of Psychoanalytic Education'. *Journal of American Psychoanalytic Association*, 34: 799–834.

Kirsner, D. (2000), *Unfree Associations*. London: Process Press.

Korda, M. (1975), *Power*. New York: Random House.

Kovel, J. (1988), *The Radical Spirit: Essays on Psychoanalysis and Society*. London: Free Association Books.

Kurtz, S. (1989), *The Art of Unknowing: Dimensions of Openness in Analytic Therapy*. New York: Jason Aronson.

Laing, R. D. (1967), *The Politics of Experience*. London: Penguin.

Laing R. D. (1970), *Knots*. London: Penguin.

Laing, R. D. (1976a), *The Politics of the Family*. London: Penguin Books.

Laing, R. D. (1976b), '*Did You Used to be R. D. Laing?* Channel 4 documentary, 1990.

Langs, R. J. (1982), *Psychotherapy: A Basic Text*. New York: Aronson.

Langs, R. J. (1988), *A Primer of Psychotherapy*. Lake Worth, FL: Gardner Press.

Langs, R. J. (1992a), *A Clinical Workbook for Psychotherapists*. London: Karnac Books.

Langs, R. J. (1992b), *Science, Systems and Psychoanalysis*. London: Karnac Books.

Bibliography

Lauer, Q. (1958), *The Triumph of Subjectivity*. New York: Fordham University Press.

Levinas, E. (1974), *En decouvrant l'éxistence avec Husserl et Heidegger* (3rd ed.). Paris: Vrin. Also in Critchley, S. (1992), *The Ethics of Deconstruction: Derrida and Levinas*. Oxford: Blackwell.

Lomas, P. (1999), *Doing Good? Psychotherapy Out of Its Depth*. Oxford: Oxford University Press.

Lomas, P. (2001), *The Limits of Interpretation* (2nd ed.). London: Constable.

McLeod, J. (2001), 'Developing a Research Tradition Consistent with the Practices and Values of Counselling and Psychotherapy'. *Counselling and Psychotherapy Research*, vol. 1, no. 1, pp. 3–11.

MacMurray, J. (1991), *The Self As Agent*. London: Faber and Faber.

MacMurray, J. (1992), *Reason and Emotion*. London: Faber and Faber.

MacMurray, J. (1995), *Persons in Relation*. London: Faber and Faber.

Macquarrie, J. (1972), *Existentialism*. London: Penguin.

Mandela, N. (1994), *Long Walk to Freedom*. London: Abacus.

Masson, J. (1984), *The Assault on Truth*. London: Penguin.

May, R. (1969), *Love and Will*. New York: Delta.

Menzies Lyth, I. (1988), *Containing Anxiety in Institutions*. London: Free Association Books.

Merleau-Ponty, M. (1962), *Phenomenology of Perception* (trans. C. Smith). London: Routledge and Kegan Paul.

Momigliano, L. N. (1992), *Shared Experience: The Psychoanalytic Dialogue*. London: Karnac Books.

Ogden, T. H. (1994), *Subjects of Analysis*. London: Karnac Books.

Ogden, T. H. (1999), *Reverie and Interpretation*. London: Karnac Books.

Oriah Mountain Dreamer (1999), *The Invitation*. London: Thorsons.

Pearce, J. C. (1977), *Magical Child*. New York: Bantam Books.

Pearmain, R. (2001), *The Heart of Listening: Attentional Qualities in Psychotherapy*. London: Continuum Books.

Phillips, A. (1988), *Winnicott*. London: Fontana.

Phillips, A. (2002), Burgh House talk to the Multi-Lingual Psychotherapy Association, 16 February 2002.

Piercy, M. (1998), *The Art of Blessing the Day*. Nottingham: Five Leaves Publications.

Pointon, C. (2002), 'Protecting the Client', *Counselling and Psychotherapy Journal*, vol. 13, no. 9, pp. 12–15.

Rank, O. (1936), *Truth and Reality*. New York: W. W. Norton and Co.

Ricoeur, P. (1991), in Valdes, M (ed.), *A Ricoeur Reader: Reflection and Imagination*. Brighton: Harvester Wheatsheaf.

Rogers, C. R. (1967), *On Becoming a Person*. London: Constable.

Rollins, H. H. (ed.) (1958), *The Letters of John Keats 1814–1821*, 2 vols. Massachusetts, CT: Harvard University Press.

Roth, A. and Fonagy, P. (1996), *What Works for Whom?: A Critical Review of Psychotherapy Research*. New York: Guilford Press.

SPC (2002), Prospectus, School of Psychotherapy and Counselling at Regent's College, London.

Saint-Exupéry, A. de (1945), *The Little Prince*, London: Piccolo.

Sampson, E. (1993), *Celebrating the Other: A Dialogic Account of Human Nature*. Hemel Hempstead: Harvester.

Schafer, R. (1976), *A New Language for Psychoanalysis*. New Haven, CT: Yale University Press.

Schafer, R. (1983), *The Analytic Attitude*. New York: Basic Books.

Schore, A. (1994), *Affect Regulation and the Origin of the Self: The Neurobiology of Emotional Development.* Hillsdale, NJ: Lawrence Erlbaum Associates.

Shakespeare, W. (1987), *Hamlet.* Oxford: Oxford University Press.

Shorter Oxford English Dictionary (1973). Oxford: Oxford University Press.

Smith, D. L. (1999), 'Communicative Psychotherapy without Tears'. In Sullivan, E. M. (ed.), *Unconscious Communication in Practice.* Buckingham: Open University Press.

Spinelli, E. (1994), *Demystifying Therapy.* London: Constable.

Spinelli, E. (1996), 'Existential-Phenomenology for the Consumer Age: The Promise and Failure of *Est*', *Journal of the Society for Existential Analysis,* vol. 7, no. 1; pp. 2–25.

Spinelli, E. (1997), *Tales of Unknowing: Therapeutic Encounters from an Existential Perspective.* London: Duckworth.

Spinelli, E. (2001), *The Mirror and the Hammer: Challenges to Therapeutic Orthodoxy.* London: Continuum Books.

Spinelli, E. and Marshall, S. (2001), *Embodied Theories.* SPC Series, London: Continuum Books.

Stanton, M. (1993), 'The Role of Psychoanalytic Studies in Psychotherapy Training', *British Journal of Psychotherapy,* vol. 10 (2), pp. 232–6.

Stern, D. (1985), *The Interpersonal World of the Infant.* New York: Basic Books.

Strong, S. R. and Claiborn, C. D. (1982), *Change through Interaction: Social Psychological Processes of Counselling and Psychotherapy.* New York: Wiley.

Sullivan, E. M. (1995), 'Shakespeare's *King Lear,* "Nature" and the Communicative Approach'. Unpublished MA thesis, SPC, Regent's College.

Sullivan, E. M. (ed.) (1999), *Unconscious Communication in Practice.* Buckingham: Open University Press.

Szasz, T. (1992), 'Taking Dialogue as Therapy Seriously: "Words Are the Essential Tool of Treatment" ', *Journal of the Society for Existential Analysis*, vol. 3, p. 3.

Tillich, P. (1960), *Love, Power and Justice*. Oxford: Oxford University Press.

Valéry, P. (1977), *An Anthology*. London: Routledge and Kegan Paul.

Viederman, M. (1991), 'The Real Person of the Analyst and his Role in the Process of Analytic Cure', Journal of Psychoanalytic Association, 39, pp. 451–89.

Wallwork, E. (1991), *Psychoanalysis and Ethics*. Newhaven: Yale University Press.

Williams, M. H. (1999), 'Psychoanalysis: An Art or a Science?' *British Journal of Psychotherapy*, vol. 16, no. 2, p. 134.

Williams, R. (2002), 'Thought for the Day', *Today*, BBC Radio 4, 11 September 2002.

Wilson, E. O. (1998), *Consilience: The Unity of Knowledge*. London: Little, Brown and Co.

Winnicott , D. W. W. (1964), *The Child, the Family and the Outside World*. London: Penguin.

Winnicott, D. W. W. (1999), *Playing and Reality*. London: Routledge.

Wood, R. E. (1969), *Martin Buber's Ontology*. Evanston: NorthWestern University Press.

Yusuf, H. (2002), 'Thought for the Day', *Today*, BBC Radio 4, 9 September 2002.

Index

Adler, A. 22
alienation, overcoming 174
anxiety 14, 15
  and conflict/disagreement 50
  students, containing 108–9
  therapists, defensive 171–2
apprenticeship model, training schools
    98
Arlow, J. 122
Arnold, M. 156
art, psychotherapy as 16–19, 23
art/technical training schools 97, 100
attending/attention 117
attitudes/qualities of
      students/therapists
  care 44, 114
  dialogic 64
  hope 56, 63, 145, 154–5
  humility 21
  insight 31, 33, 95, 128
  love 22, 24, 113, 148, 149
  openness 10, 11, 19, 20, 24, 26–9,
    77, 112, 182
  respect 145, 152
  self-awareness 10, 27–30, 39
  self-confidence 80, 119
  self-consciousness 67, 78, 80
  self-critical attitude 102
  spontaneity 80, 81
  see also therapeutic relationship
autonomy, individual 25, 145
  issues for students 35–6
Aveline, M. 166

British Association for Counselling
    and Psychotherapy (BACP) 93

Baranger, M. 82, 83
Baranger, W. 82, 83
Bateson, G. 88
Bauman, Z. 74
being-there (dasein) 65, 66, 69
Being There, Peter Sellers 65
being-together
  as basis of therapy 68, 69, 74–9,
    121, 166
  failure 83
  impact of therapists feelings 81–3,
    146
  teacher/student 83–4
  therapist/client 9, 11, 24, 65–84
  transference/real relationship
    79–84
  see also therapeutic relationship
being-with-the-other, see other
being-with-others in training, see
    group work
Bergin, A. E. 166
between 4, 68, 75, 76
  see also intersubjective approach;
    spirit/soul
Binswanger, L. 76, 144
Bion, W. R. 81, 122, 128, 169
bipersonal field 82–3
birth/death metaphor of learning 53,
    55
Bleger, J. 97, 108
body language 12
body/mind split 124
Bollas, C. 80
Boss, M. 9, 69
boundaries, establishing therapeutic
    38, 39, 132

Index

Bowlby, J. 22
British Psychological Society (BPS)
  93
Buber, M. 3, 4, 6, 9, 20, 23, 50, 51,
  56, 64, 66, 67, 68, 74, 76, 78,
  119, 121, 146, 158, 181
Burns, R. 179

Cambridge Society of Psychotherapy
  105
Campart, M. 116
Capra, F. 82
care, attitude of
  therapists 44
  training organizations 114
caring, motives 24–5, 151–3, 159,
  160
case studies 133–4
Christian values 2, 25
chrysalis analogy 10, 102, 107,
  109–10
Claiborn, C. D. 59
clinical placement 130–1
clinical psychology 16
collaboration
  authors 2–4, 7, 12–13, 70–1,
    165, 181–2
  teachers 114
  see also dialogic model/dialogue
Coltart, N. 80
communication, see dialogic
  model/dialogue
confidentiality 161–3
conflict/disagreement 49–51, 63, 84
  learning to cope with 129, 130
connection, see being-together;
  meeting
containment of unpredictability
  38–9
  see also holding
conversation 46–8, 77
  see also dialogic model/dialogue
counselling, see psychotherapy

cradling metaphor 44, 64
  see also holding; safe-enough
    environment
creativity 24, 63, 174
  self discovery through 109
Critchley, S. 70
criticism, tolerating 49, 50
Cupitt, D. 173

dasein/daseinalysis, see being-there
defensiveness 175, 176
  teachers 60, 61, 103, 109, 157
dialogic model of teaching/learning 8,
    9, 23, 26, 45–64, 83, 103, 146
  as attitude 64
  and conflict/disagreement 49–51,
    63, 84
  and conversation 46–8, 77
  costs/drawbacks 179
  and intimacy, interpersonal 49
  and learning 53–6
  and response 45–6
  as subversive 178–80
  dialogue 45–52, 63, 77
difference-sameness, accepting
    69–70, 71, 79, 163–4, 171
disagreement/conflict 49, 50, 51, 63,
    84
dissertations 137
dualism 124
duty, devaluation 25

education, problem-posing 63
empathy 71, 120, 122
encounter, see meeting, therapeutic
  see also being-together; therapeutic
    relationship
engagement, in therapeutic
  relationship 21, 49
enlightenment 15, 25
environment, learning 31
ethical issues in training/therapy 2, 6,
    11, 12, 25, 144–64

Index

codes 93–5, 101
confidentiality/ disclosure 161–3
defining 145
power 146–52
professional neutrality 24, 81, 113,
  149
and responsibility 144–5, 154,
  155–9, 160
self-deception/truthfulness
  159–61, 162
supervision 159, 161–3
teaching 157–8
evaluation, students 33–4, 102–5,
  138–9, 159
qualifications/measurement
  99–100, 104
existential-phenomenological
  approach to psychotherapy 6, 9,
  73, 104
expertise, avoiding concept 57, 61,
  100, 145, 170

failure
  being-together 83
  to learn/teach 139–41
  legislating against 95
  management 102–5
  students, ethics 159
  therapy 133
Fairbairn, R. 22, 44, 80
fees, charging 34, 35, 92
fear, overcoming 150, 175, 176
Ferenczi, S. 21
  'Confusion of Tongues' 21
Figlio, K. 90, 94, 98, 101
Fonagy, P. 166
Frankl, V. 6, 22–3
freedom/security 15
  see also autonomy
Freire, P. 8, 45, 56, 63
Freud, S. 14, 21, 95, 98, 136, 160,
  178
Freudian slips 160

Fromm, E. 15, 22
Fromm-Reichmann, F. 76

Gadamer, H. -G. 116
Gans, S. 92, 98, 99
Garfield, S. L. 166
gender issues 7
globalization 86
Goldenberg, H. 20, 28, 47, 68, 106,
  121, 146
good-enough therapist 112
Gordon, P. 17, 91, 116, 118, 123,
  151, 169, 171, 172, 177
Grayling, A. C. 147
group work, in learning 129–30
Güggenbühl-Craig, A. 24, 151, 163

Hale, N. G. 160
Hamlet 154
health/healing, mental 14
  therapeutic relationship in
    facilitating 21, 68, 69, 74–9,
    121, 166
hearing 158
  music analogy 117–18
  see also listening
Heidegger, M. 57, 65, 116, 144
helping, motives 151–3, 159, 160
Hillel, 144
Hockney, D. 100
holding 20, 22, 24, 44, 51, 64, 106,
  108–9
  see also safe-enough environment
holism/wholism 18, 19, 158, 168
Holloway, R. 161
homelessness metaphor 106–7, 179
human rights 156
humility, towards client 21

I-Thou stance 67, 74, 76, 158
  see also being-together; meeting
Ignatieff, M. 167
Illich, I. 91

individual autonomy 25, 145
indoctrination 37, 83
insight 31, 33, 95, 128
integrative stance 88, 89, 171
intersubjective approach 3, 4, 9, 21, 73, 158
    teaching 45
    see also between; dialogic model
intimacy, interpersonal 49
Isaacson, Z. 47, 68, 121, 146

journey, therapy 20
Judaism 153, 176
    ethical 2, 6
    intolerance 25

Kennedy, R, 80, 81
Kernberg, O. 97, 98
King Lear 106, 147, 179
Kirsner, D. 98, 99
Kleinian perspective 22
knowing 121–2, 124
    see also unknowing
Korda, M. 36
Kovel, J. 86, 87
Kurtz, S. 171, 172

Laing, R. D. 6, 19, 23, 42, 43, 68–9, 72, 73, 83, 96, 121, 158
Langs, R. 23, 82
language, psychotherapeutic 166, 167, 171
Lauer, Q. 54
learning 52–6
    atmosphere, creating 41
    birth/death metaphor 53, 55
    brain structure 52
    community 105–10
        see also training organizations
    incremental nature 53–4
    rhythms 39, 40, 52–3, 115–16, 119
    un-learning 55, 100, 112
    see also students

Levinas, E. 73, 79, 144
liberation education 8, 9
    see also dialogic model
listening 115, 116, 158, 176–7
    see also vigilant passivity
Lomas, P. 18, 80, 81, 153
love, in therapeutic relationship 22, 24, 113, 148, 149

McLeod, J. 19, 135
MacMurray, J. 16, 17, 40, 51, 119, 157, 181
Macquarrie, J. 173
Mandela, N. 150, 176
Marshall, S. 170
Maslow, A. 154
May, R. 76
meeting, therapeutic 68, 69, 74–9, 120–1, 166
    see also being-together; therapeutic relationship
mentorship 7, 8, 11, 37, 57, 170
Menziez Lyth, I. 108
Merleau-Ponty, M. 49
mind/body split 124
mindfulness 176
Momigliano, L. N. 26
motives, for training as psychotherapist 24–5, 151–3, 159, 160
mystery, psychotherapy 31, 33, 42–3, 182
    understanding 95
mystic experiences, *see* spirit/soul

neutrality, professional 24, 81, 113, 149
    absence of 81–3, 146
Nietzsche, F. W. 150

object-relations school 5, 22
observational powers 6
Ogden, T. H. 81, 119, 128

openness of mind 10, 11, 19, 20, 24, 26–9, 77, 112, 182
optimism 145, 154–5
organizations, *see* training organizations
Oriah Mountain Dreamer 159, 161, 162
other
  encounter with 19, 24, 66–9, 72–3, 80, 121, 164
  openness to 10, 11, 19, 20, 24, 77, 182
  responsibility 73–4
  same/difference 69–70, 71, 79, 163–4, 171
  teachers/learners 70–1

parental relationships 22
Pearce, J. C. 52, 53
Pearmain, R. 14, 18, 117, 170
personal communion 16
personal development essays, student 134–5
phenomenological approach
  to psychotherapy 6, 9, 73
  in teaching 104–5
Phillips, A. 49
placements, clinical 130–1
power 146–52
  asymmetry 64, 145, 161
  and caring 151, 152
  training organizations 33, 36–8, 102, 105, 107, 114
  will to 149, 150, 151
powerlessness feelings 1, 14, 15, 87
presence 76–9
problem-posing education 63
process reports, student 133–4
professionalism 155
  neutrality 24, 81, 113, 149
  see also statutory registration
professionalization of psychotherapy 10, 177
  dangers 174

psychiatry 16
psychoanalysis, *see* psychotherapy
psychology, clinical 16
psychotherapists, qualities, *see* attitudes/qualities
psychotherapy
  art and science 16–19, 23
  defining 5, 8, 16, 24
  demystifying 31, 33, 42–3
  fees 34, 35, 92
  founding fathers 21–3
  integration of different schools 88, 89, 171
  limitations 172–3, 177
  professionalization 10, 174, 177
  social context 85–8
  status 17, 170
  for students 141–3
  success 166, 173
  technique, secondary importance of 21, 22
  see also statutory registration; therapeutic relationship

qualifications, impact on training 99–100, 104

Rank, O. 159, 160
rapport 68–9
  see also being-together; between; intersubjective approach
reading 125–6
reality testing 32
Redler, L. 92, 98, 99
reflective capacity 81, 87, 127–8
Regent's College, School of Psychotherapy and Counselling 107
relationships 173–8
  children's 175
  defensiveness in 23, 175, 176
  dialogic stance in 174–5
  parental 22

relationships (*cont.*)
    sanctification of the everyday 176
    students/training organizations 97, 101
    therapeutic attitude in 175, 176
    see also therapeutic relationship
religious faith, loss 156, 157
religious seminary model, training organizations 98, 100
repairing the world 152–4
    see also caring
research, student 135–6
respectfulness 145, 152
responsibility
    other 144–5, 154, 155–9, 160
    self 145, 160
    training organizations 33, 36–8, 102, 105, 107, 114
reverie, intersubjective 127
rhythms of learning 39, 40, 52–3, 115–16, 119
Ricoeur, P. 72
rights, human 156
Rogers, C. R. 55
role-play, student 126–7
Roth, A. 166
rule-breaking 160

Schafer, R. 80
safe-enough environment 10, 102, 107, 109–10 *see also* holding
Saint-Exupéry, A. 112
sameness-difference, accepting 69–70, 71, 79, 163–4, 171
Sampson, E. 46
schizophrenia 22, 23
schools, psychotherapy
    see training organizations
Schore, A. 52
science, psychotherapy as 16–19, 23
Searles, Harold 23
security 15

selection processes 101–2, 112–14
    diverse candidates 102
    see also attitudes/qualities of students/therapists
self-awareness, developing 10, 27–30, 39
self-confidence, therapists 80, 119
self-consciousness, therapists 67, 78, 80
self-deception/truthfulness 159–61, 162
self-development, and psychotherapy 87
self-reflective capacity, therapists/students 81, 87, 102, 114, 127–8
self-restraint, learning 119, 148, 150, 151
Shakespeare, W.
    Hamlet 154
    King Lear 106, 147, 179
Shapiro, D. A. 166
skills practice 126–7
social alienation, overcoming 174
social context, psychotherapy 85–8
Spinelli, E. 23, 31, 73, 79, 122, 166, 170
spirit/soul 68, 75, 76
    communion 73
splitting 22
spontaneity, therapeutic relationship 80, 81
Stanton, M. 101, 123
status issues 17, 170
statutory registration 88–96
    advantages 92–6
    codes of ethics 93–5, 101
    see also ethical issues in training/therapy
    dangers/limitations 90–5
    legislating against failure 95
    and self-regulation 94
Stern, D. 52

Strong, S. R. 59
students
  attitudes see attitudes/qualities of
    students/therapists
  failure, *see* failure
  personal development essays 134–5
  personal therapy 141–3
  process reports/client studies
    133–4
  research 135–6
  risks 27, 28
  selection, *see* selection processes
  supervision, *see* supervision
  self-interest 113–14
  therapeutic aspects for 11, 26,
    27–30
  trust/autonomy issues 35–6
  writing 133
subversion 178–80
Sullivan, E. M. 147
Sullivan, H. S. 21–2
supervision 131–3
  ethical issues 161–3
  perspectives 131, 132
syllabus 166
Szasz, T. 152

Talmud 125, 157
teachers 56–62
  collaborative approach 114
  competence 32
  defensiveness 60, 61, 103, 109,
    157
  dialogic style 60, 61, 62
  as models 7, 8, 11, 37, 57–8, 61,
    170
  non-authoritative 57, 61, 100
  as performers 58–60
  as practitioners 57
  professional development 32
  qualities 56, 57, 63–4
  as representatives of training
    organization 97, 102, 108

teaching, *see* training
theory
  avoidance of indoctrination 168,
    171, 179
  integrative stance 88, 89, 171
  limitations 170, 171, 172
  uses 11, 20, 21, 30, 123
  value 166–70, 171
therapeutic dyad 82–3
  see also being-together; therapeutic
    relationship
therapeutic encounter, *see* meeting,
    therapeutic
  see also being-together; therapeutic
    relationship
therapeutic relationship 15, 19, 55
  asymmetry 64, 145, 161
  as healing factor 21, 68, 69, 74–9,
    121, 166
  love 22, 24, 113, 148, 149
  parallels with teacher/learner
    relationship 8, 26–30, 49, 61
  professionally neutral 24, 81, 113,
    149
  and 'real' relationships 79, 80
  reciprocity/mutuality 145–6
  and transference relationship
    79–84
  see also attitudes/qualities of
    students/therapists; being-
    together
therapy, *see* psychotherapy
therapy industry 99
therapy training, *see* training
thinking 123–4
Tillich, P. 145, 146, 148, 149
trainees, *see* students
training organizations 10, 96–110
  care, attitude 114
  closed shops 99
  dialogic approach 103
  evaluation, *see* evaluation
  expert model 100, 145

failure management *see* failure
indoctrination 37, 83
learning community 105–10
models 97–100
phenomenological approach
    104–5
relationships with students 97, 101
responsibilities/powers 33, 36–8,
    102, 105, 107, 114
selection processes 101–2, 112–14
teachers as representatives 97, 102,
    108
training, psychotherapeutic 5, 30–3,
    111–14
best practice 30
boundaries 38, 39
clinical placement 130–1
contextualizing 85–110
contract 30, 31
early stages 114–16
effectiveness feedback 31
evaluation 33–4, 138–9, 159
failure, *see* failure
funding issues 34–5
intersubjective approach 45
manipulative quality 59, 60
mentoring element 7, 8, 11, 37,
    57, 170
parallels with practice 8, 26–30,
    49, 61
qualifications, impact 99–100, 104
reality testing 32
specific skills 27–30, 39, 116–30
structure 30–6
time-frame 32
see also learning; students; training
    organizations
transference/real relationships 79–84
truth 159–61, 162
competing 72

quest for 80

unconscious
    discovery 155
    rationalizations 160
understanding/insight 31, 33, 95,
    128
United Kingdom Council for
    Psychotherapy (UKCP) 90, 93
university model, training
    organizations 98–101
unknowing 23, 79, 119, 122–4, 128,
    139
    tolerating 179, 180
un-learning 55, 100, 112

Valéry, P. 168
validation/non-validation 23
values, societal 2, 6, 25
    see also ethical issues
vicious cycles, repeating 83
vigilant passivity 5, 10, 100
    see also listening

waiting 118–19
Wallwork, E. 161
wholism 18, 19, 158, 168
will to power 149, 150, 151
Williams, M. H. 116
Wilson, E. O. 17, 19
    'Ionian Enchantment' 17
Winnicott, Donald Woods 22, 44,
    80, 96, 109, 119
'with-world' existentialism 9
witnessing 120
writing 133
Wood, R. E. 76

Yusuf, H. 168